Partnership working with family carers of people with a learning disability and people with autism

Series Editor: Lesley Barcham

Mandatory Unit and Common Induction Standards titles

Communicating effectively with people with a learning disability
ISBN 978 0 85725 510 5

Personal development for learning disability workers ISBN 978 0 85725 609 6

Equality and inclusion for learning disability workers ISBN 978 0 85725 514 3

Duty of care for learning disability workers ISBN 978 0 85725 613 3

Principles of safeguarding and protection for learning disability workers
ISBN 978 0 85725 506 8

Person centred approaches when supporting people with a learning disability
ISBN 978 0 85725 625 6

The role of the learning disability worker ISBN 978 0 85725 637 9

Handling information for learning disability workers ISBN 978 0 85725 633 1

Health and safety for learning disability workers ISBN 978 0 85725 641 6

Titles supporting a unit from the level 2 health and social care qualifications

An introduction to supporting people with autistic spectrum conditions
ISBN 978 0 85725 710 7

An introduction to supporting people with a learning disability
ISBN 978 0 85725 709 3

Titles supporting a unit from the level 3 health and social care qualifications

Promoting positive behaviour when supporting people with a learning disability and people with autism ISBN 978 0 85725 713 0

Next steps in supporting people with autistic spectrum conditions
ISBN 978 0 85275 705 5

Partnership working with family carers of people with a learning disability and people with autism ISBN 978 1 905218240

Partnership working with family carers of people with a learning disability and people with autism

Alison Cowen and Jamie Hanson

Supporting a unit from the level 3 health and social care qualifications

Acknowledgements

Our thanks to Robina Mallett and Hft Family Carer Support Services for their contribution to the production of this book, and to Warwickshire Quality Partnership and Liz Jones.

Photographs from www.crockstockimages.com, www.careimages.com and www.shutterstock.com. Our thanks to James and Tina Cooper, Marianne and Choices Housing.

First published in 2013 by the British Institute of Learning Disabilities

All rights reserved. No part of this publication may be reproduced, stored in a retrieval system, or transmitted in any form or by any means, electronic, mechanical, photocopying, recording, or otherwise, without prior permission in writing from BILD.

© 2013 BILD

British Library Cataloguing in Publication Data
A CIP record for this book is available from the British Library
ISBN: 978 1 905218 240
The right of Alison Cowen and Jamie Hanson to be identified as the authors of this Work has been asserted by them in accordance with the Copyright, Designs and Patents Act 1988.

Cover design by Pentacor
Text design by Pentacor
Typeset by Mark Heslington
Printed and bound in Great Britain by Latimer Trend and Company Ltd, Plymouth

BILD
Campion House
Green Street
Kidderminster
Worcestershire
DY10 1JL
Tel: 01562 723010
www.bild.org.uk

Contents

About the authors and the people who contributed to this book	vii
Introduction	ix
Chapter 1: Setting the scene	1
Chapter 2: Understanding partnership working with families	21
Chapter 3: Establishing and maintaining positive relationships with families	45
Chapter 4: Planning shared approaches to the care and support of individuals with families	63
Chapter 5: Working with families to enable them to access support in their role as carers	86
Chapter 6: Recording and sharing information together – is the partnership working?	106
Glossary	119
Index	122

This book covers:

- The Level 3 health and social care unit HSC 3038 – Work in partnership with families to support individuals

About the authors and the people who contributed to this book

This book has been written by Alison Cowen and Jamie Hanson with the assistance of a number of additional contributors whose stories and experiences provide real life examples.

Alison Cowen

Alison is a freelance writer and has a son aged 33 who has a place of his own and support from a team including four personal assistants (PAs) organised through a personal budget. A major theme of Alison's work is about empowering families to see the gifts and abilities of their disabled children and young people through information and example. This encourages them to aim high in becoming active citizens in their communities with the support that they need.

Jamie Hanson

Through his work with disabled people and families, Jamie has transformed the lives of hundreds of people by enabling them to take control, plan and organise the personalised support they need to live their chosen life. In addition, Jamie has trained numerous professionals and family members in support planning using his personal skills and expertise in neuro linguistic programming. When working with people, Jamie always promotes family leadership and focuses on the essence or uniqueness of each person as a starting point for support planning. Jamie admits that he always learns as much from the people he supports as they do from him.

The many family contributors to this book come from a variety of backgrounds and cultures. Some of them have asked to remain anonymous. One thing they share in common is a desire and commitment to achieve the best possible support for their family member so that they can enjoy a fulfilling life. In the process of organising great support for their own son or daughter, brother sister or cousin, many recognise that they have also changed things for the better for other disabled people and their families.

Our contributors include:

Frank and Judi Lunt

who worked with a support organisation to get the best possible support for their daughter. The organisation learnt from this experience and has made significant changes to the way it operates.

Kausar Iqbal and Lynne Bailey

who have passed their experiences as family members on to other families through setting up the organisation, Beeston Action for Families www.beestonactionforfamilies.org.uk

Pauline Rogers

whose daughter, Alison, now has her own shared ownership home and is enjoying supported living, after many other different living arrangements over the years. Pauline says: 'Since Alison moved into her own home two years ago her quality of life, her confidence and independence have grown more than I could possibly have expected. She is a role-model for other people with learning disabilities and I am hugely proud of her. All the hard work it has taken to finally achieve this has been so worth it.'

Other contributors are paid workers who appreciate and value the importance of supporting people in the context of their family. They include **Sarah Holdstock**, **Maja Koch**, and **Richard Wood** who is also a family member. Many have found the journey to partnership working challenging and yet often speak of how rewarding a successful partnership can be for the person, the family and themselves.

Introduction

Who is this book for?

Partnership Working with Family Carers of People with a Learning Disability and People with Autism is for you if you:

- want to learn how to work positively with family carers to provide quality support;

- want to understand the experiences and perspectives of family carers;

- work in health or social care with people with a learning disability or autism;

- are a manager in a service supporting people with a learning disability or people with autism and have training or supervisory responsibility for the development of your staff;

- are a personal assistant and are employed by an individual with disabilities and/or their family carers.

Links to assessment

If you are studying for this unit and want to gain accreditation towards a qualification, first of all you will need to make sure that you are registered with an awarding organisation which offers the qualification. Then you will need to provide a portfolio of evidence for assessment. The person responsible for training within your organisation will advise you about registering with an awarding organisation and give you information about the type of evidence you will need to provide for assessment. You can also get additional information from BILD. For more information about qualifications and assessment, go to the BILD website: www.bild.org.uk/qualifications

How this book is organised

Generally each chapter covers one learning outcome from the qualification unit. The learning outcomes covered are clearly highlighted at the beginning of each chapter. Each chapter starts with a story from a person with a learning disability or family carer or worker. This introduces the topic and is intended to help you think about the topic from their point of view. Each chapter contains:

Thinking points – to help you reflect on your practice;

Stories – examples of good support from people with learning disabilities and family carers;

Activities – for you to use to help you to think about your work with people with learning disabilities;

Key points – a summary of the main messages in that chapter;

References and where to go for more information – useful references to help further study.

At the end of the book there is:

A glossary – explaining specialist language in plain English;

An index – to help you look up a particular topic easily.

Study skills

Studying for a qualification can be very rewarding. However, it can be daunting if you have not studied for a long time, or are wondering how to fit your studies into an already busy life. The BILD website contains lots of advice to help you to study successfully, including information about effective reading, taking notes, organising your time, and using the internet for research. For further information, go to www.bild.org.uk/qualifications

Chapter 1
Setting the scene

Angie's story

When Angie left home we, as her parents, were closely involved in recruiting and training a committed team of paid staff to support her. Six months on and Angie is happy and enjoying her new home and her new life. It wouldn't have worked so well if we hadn't been involved from the start – we know Angie – we knew what would make it work, what makes her happy and what makes her sad. And we knew what was important to her and what she wanted to achieve in the future.

Our trusting relationship with Angie's paid staff has been built on a shared desire to create the best possible support for her. Her family's contribution to her support was important because she would not have been able to direct her own support independently.

Frank, Angie's dad

Introduction

This book focuses on good practice in working in partnership with families. It is important to remember that each individual that you support is unique with their own likes, dislikes, dreams, hopes, fears, skills, memories and experiences. In the same way, each family is different and their various relationships are equally unique.

In this introductory chapter we explore the different terms used to describe family carers and explain why it is important to take your lead from the people you work with. The chapter gives an overview of the key UK legislation and policies related to support for people with a learning disability, support for people with autism and working with and involving family carers. The key values and principles underpinning effective work with family carers are discussed and the chapter concludes by exploring the changes for people and their families as a result of personalisation and self directed support.

Learning outcomes

This chapter will help you to:

- understand what is meant by the terms carer, family carer and family members and think about how families are involved with and contribute to the lives of their sons, daughters, siblings or other relatives with a learning disability or autism;

- understand the policy context for the support of family carers and people with a learning disability and people with autism in the four countries of the UK;

- identify the values that promote effective working with families including the Skills for Care and Skills for Health common core principles;

- understand how the development of self directed support and personalisation affect the role of family members.

This chapter covers:

- Level 3 HSC 3038 – Work in partnership with families to support individuals – a background introduction to learning outcomes 1–5

Understanding who we mean by family members

Thinking point

Think about your own family and other families that you know. How do family members relate to each other and express their feelings, views and emotions? What makes each family unique?

> To work effectively with people with learning disabilities I need to find out about who they are, and who their families are or who they are surrounded by. I need to know who and what has made them the person they are. I need to be able to relate to their environment including their parents or other family members. Without it I can't do my work.
>
> *Maja Koch, Support worker*

To work effectively with a person with a learning disability you need to find out about who they are, who their family are and who they are surrounded by.

Many parents, siblings and other relatives of people with learning disabilities and people with autism see themselves as just that – their son or daughter's mum or dad, the person's brother, sister, aunt, uncle or grandparent. They may dislike the label 'carer' or 'family carer', whilst recognising that in order to receive services this is how they need to portray themselves.

The National Family Carer Network gives an explanation of the term family carer, it highlights that the key factors in relation to a family carer is:

- they have a personal experience of supporting a family member who has a learning disability;

- the person may be at home or living away from home;
- the person is not paid to have a relationship with the person with a learning disability;
- their relationship with the person with a learning disability is personal and continuous.

The National Family Carer Network says:

> A family carer has personal experience of caring for a family member who has a learning disability, even if that individual has moved away from home. A family carer is a person who is *not paid* to have a personal, continuous relationship with a person with a learning disability.
>
> *From www.familycarers.org.uk*

Many family members dislike the term 'carer', even though it is the term used in most policies and government guidance, because it suggests a particular kind of relationship in which tasks are done 'to' rather than 'with' someone. They may prefer to talk about 'supporting' their son or daughter rather than 'caring' for them. For others, 'carer' implies a paid carer and does not reflect their relationship or experience. In fact many would define their own family in a broader way that includes grandparents, cousins, friends and neighbours who are close to them. The term family member is therefore seen as being a more neutral term and it is therefore the term used in this book.

Rather than automatically using terms which come from services, policy or legislation and which may carry negative connotations it is respectful to ask family members what they themselves prefer to be called. As one family member said: 'We love ordinary!'

The caring role in policy

In *The National Carers Strategy: Carers at the Heart of the 21st Century Families and Communities* (2008), the Department of Health, in their policy for carers in England, defined the role of carers as follows:

> A carer spends a significant proportion of their life providing unpaid support to family or potentially friends. This could be caring for a relative, partner or friend who is ill, frail, disabled or has mental health or substance misuse problems.

The strategy identified the importance of the role of carers and how this has been underestimated and undervalued in the past. In moving forward, the Strategy set out a vision that by 2018:

> Carers will be universally recognised and valued as being fundamental to strong families and stable communities. Support will be tailored to meet individuals' needs, enabling carers to maintain a balance between their caring responsibilities and a life outside caring, while enabling the person they support to be a full and equal citizen.
>
> In addition, it is important to recognise that carers come from diverse backgrounds including age, gender, race, religious belief, disability and sexual orientation.

One of the five intended outcomes of the National Carers Strategy is that:

> Carers will be respected as **expert care partners** and will have access to the integrated and personalised services they need to support them in their caring role.

Although government policy acknowledges the unique contribution of family carers and that they should be respected as expert care partners the reality in some situations is that carers and family members have felt that they have been excluded from involvement in the decisions about the support needed by or provided to their family member, or that their views or opinions have been ignored. The Mencap Report *Death by Indifference* (2007) described how the avoidable deaths of six individuals with learning disabilities could have been prevented through equal access to appropriate healthcare. A common theme in the report was how the parents and families of each individual were not listened to or included in decisions about care and treatment.

In response to the *Death by Indifference* report, an independent inquiry was established with Sir Jonathan Michael as its Chair. In the report *Healthcare for All* (2008) it was reported that family carers of adults with learning disabilities

> … often find their opinions and assessments ignored by healthcare professionals, even though they often have the best information about, and understanding of, the people they support. They struggle to be accepted as effective partners in care by those involved in providing general healthcare; their complaints are not heard; they are expected to do too much of the care that should be provided by the health system and are often required to provide care beyond their personal resources. (Department of Health, 2008)

Thinking point

What might this failure to work in effective partnership mean for family members and for people with learning disabilities and people with autism? How could you promote effective partnership working?

The policy context of working in partnership with families

It is now accepted that people with learning disabilities and people with autism have from time to time received poorer quality support because service providers and professionals have ignored the expertise and knowledge of families. Recent legislation and policy guidance has recognised the contribution and expertise of families and working in partnership with family members is positively encouraged. The table below lists the key policies and guidance for the four UK countries, including those on learning disability, autism, family carers and personalisation.

Key legislation and guidance relating to the family carers and support for people with autism and people with a learning disability

ENGLAND
Published by Department of Health www.dh.gov.uk

Valuing People (2001) and **Valuing People Now (2009)**

Families are recognised and valued in *Valuing People Now* (2009). It emphasised that:

'Families are at the heart of *Valuing People Now*. When we use the term "family" we are including everyone in the family; including people with learning disabilities. No two families are the same and they come in all shapes and sizes but when we speak to families most of them tell us that three things are very important:

- getting the best life possible for their family member with a learning disability;
- for other people to recognise and value the role of families and to work in partnership with them; and
- for family carers to get the help and support they need to live a good life.'

(From April 2011 responsibility for the strategy passed to local authority social services departments.)

The Autism Act (2009) – the first ever disability-specific law in England. It put a duty on the government to produce a strategy for adults with autism; *Fulfilling and Rewarding Lives. The Strategy for Adults with Autism in England* was published in 2010.

Fulfilling and Rewarding lives: The Strategy for Adults with Autism (2010) – The strategy placed a duty on the government to produce statutory guidance for local councils and local health bodies. It aims to make fundamental changes in public services to help adults with autism live independent lives including finding work. The strategy sets a clear framework for all mainstream services across the public sector to work together for adults with autism.

The National Carers Strategy: Carers at the Heart of the 21st Century Families and Communities (2008) – (see above)

A Vision for Adult Social Care: Capable Communities and Active Citizens (2010) – sets out how the Government wishes to see services delivered for people in England and provides a new direction for adult social care, with personalised services and outcomes as central. It builds on seven principles including personalisation – where individuals and their families can take control of their care and develop a new partnership between individuals, communities, the voluntary and statutory sectors and the NHS.

Think Local, Act Personal (2010) – a commitment to delivering personalisation and community-based support; building on what has already been achieved with *Putting People First*. It explains how councils, health bodies, providers and other community organisations will work more closely so that individuals, their families and carers have greater choice and control over their care and support. It recognises the contribution that individuals, families and communities make in providing care and support – both to those who are publicly funded and those who either pay for themselves or rely on family carers. It sets the scene for the way forward for personalisation and community-based support.

Carers Recognition and Services Act (1995) – covers carers' assessments and recognising sustainability of carer's input as a crucial element in community care law.

Carers and Disabled Children Act (2000) – consideration for services for carers in their own right.

Carers (Equal Opportunities) Act (2004) – includes recognition of carers rights to employment, education and leisure issues in assessing needs.

Work and Families Act (2006) – includes the ability to request flexible working and time off for caring responsibilities (via Employment Relations Act 1999).

Assessment Directions (2004) – includes the right to be consulted during the assessment of a cared for person.

Children and Young Persons Act (2008) – provision of short breaks for parent carers.

Equality Act (2010) – covers protection from discrimination arising because of association with a disabled person (or a person with any other characteristic protected under equality law).

WALES
Published by Welsh Government www.wales.gov.uk

Statement on Policy and Practice for Adults with a Learning Disability (Wales 2007) – covers the key areas of advocacy; person centred planning, transition, day opportunities, employment, accommodation and independence.

Sustainable Social Services for Wales – A Framework for Action (2011) – sets out the Government's plans to renew social services and social care for the next decade.

The Autistic Spectrum Disorder Strategic Action Plan for Wales (2008) – this was the first time guidelines specific to autism and Asperger syndrome were set out for local authorities to follow in Wales. The plan also outlines what the Welsh Government has to do in order to meet the needs of people with autism and their families. It covers everyone on the autism spectrum in Wales, including people with Asperger syndrome.

SCOTLAND
Published by Scottish Executive www.scotland.gov.uk

The Same as You? A Review of Services for People with Learning Disabilities (2000) – a national implementation group worked with service providers, people with a learning disability, family carers and local authorities to highlight the need for services to be developed to better meet the needs of the increased number of people living in the community. People with a learning disability should be provided with support that allows them to live a normal life, living in their own home or a homely setting with adequate support to allow them to live as independently as possible, through a flexible, person-centred support package. It promotes a person-centred approach to services ensuring people with learning disabilities are involved in making choices about what they want.

The Scottish Strategy for Autism (2011) – in 2008 Scotland produced *Commissioning Services for People on the Autism Spectrum: Policy and Practice Guidance* to inform those commissioning health and social care services for people with autism. In 2010 *Towards an Autism Strategy for Scotland* was published for consultation. The *Scottish Strategy for Autism* was launched in 2011. The purpose of this plan is to provide direction for the development of services by ensuring that specific and measurable actions are undertaken and, on the basis of evidence of prevalence and need, commissioning interagency services at local, regional or national levels as appropriate.

Self Directed Support: A National Strategy for Scotland (2011) – a 10 year strategy for self-directed support in Scotland which aims to set out and drive a cultural shift around providing support that views people as equal citizens with rights and responsibilities. The vision for Scotland is that:

- the lives of people who require support are enriched through greater independence, control, and choice that lead to improved health and well being, and the best outcomes possible;
- self-directed support should become the mainstream mechanism for the delivery of social care support. Building on the success of direct payments, every person eligible for statutory services should be able to make a genuinely informed choice and have a clear and transparent allocation of resources allowing them to decide how best to meet their needs;
- choice should be available to all, but imposed on no-one.

NORTHERN IRELAND
Published by Northern Ireland Assembly, Department of Health and Social Services and Public Safety www.dhsspsni.gov.uk

Review of Mental Health and Learning Disability (Northern Ireland). Equal Lives: Review of Policy and Services for People with a Learning disability in Northern Ireland (2005) – this review is based on the five key values of: citizenship; social inclusion; empowerment; working together; and individual support. Under working together the review says, 'Conditions must be created where people with a learning disability, families, and organisations work well together in order to meet the needs and aspirations of people with a learning disability … The role of family carers as partners in these processes should be recognised and valued.'

The Autism Act (Northern Ireland) (2011) – it states that the Department of Health, Social Services and Public Safety has to prepare a strategy on autism that must be published in not less than two years after the passing of this Act.

Transforming Your Care (TYC) consultation (2012) – the Northern Ireland Assembly is consulting on a transformation programme for health and social care. The review proposed a model of health and social care which would drive the future shape and direction of the service and put the **individual at the centre** with services becoming increasingly accessible in local areas. This transformation will result in a significant shift in the way services are provided across hospitals and the community, with some provision moving from hospitals to the community, where it is safe and effective to do this.

Some of the key messages from these policies and legislations are:

- Families should be recognised and valued. Family members are equal support partners, many have become experts with skills and knowledge that are to be valued and appreciated.

- Working in an equal partnership with family members is important to ensure good support.

- Family carers often have knowledge and skills that can be shared to ensure their family member gets good support. Family carers can have skills they need to acquire.

- Respect and recognise that family members will have their own support needs, they should get the help and support they need to live a good life.

- It should not be assumed that carers are 'willing and able' to provide care and support; they have the right to have their needs assessed and services provided to them; they should have equal rights to work, training and leisure opportunities and not be discriminated against through association with a disabled person.

Core principles for working with families

Over the last 10 years working well in partnership with family carers has become a priority in government policies. Skills for Care and Skills for Health were asked to produce training resources to help services and individual workers to develop the skills and knowledge to work in partnership with carers and families. As part of *Carers Matter – Everybody's Business* (2011), they have developed a national (England) set of common core principles for working with carers. The principles are intended to be the foundation upon which good practice is built. They are intended to reinforce, challenge and help change practice when working with family carers.

The eight principles are:

1. Carers are equal partners in care. Recognise that over time, carers become experts with skills that are to be valued and appreciated.

2. Make no assumptions regarding a carer's capacity or carers' capacities and willingness to take responsibility for or to continue to care.

3. Support carers to be as physically and mentally as well as possible and prevent ill health.

4. Work together to involve all carers in decision making and choices at all levels and at all stages in the caring role in a positive, timely and proactive way, following best practice in sharing information.

5. Provide care and support with flexibility and understanding in a personalised way that reflects the circumstances, cultural background and lifestyle of the carer and the person cared for.

6. Respect and recognise that carers will have their own support needs, rights and aspirations which may be different from that of the cared for person.

7. Identify, support and enable children and young people who are carers to be children and young people as well as carers.

8. Recognise the experience of carers as the caring role ends and after it has ended and offer support to carers accordingly.

Carers are equal partners in care. Recognise that over time, carers become experts with skills that are to be valued and appreciated.

> ### Activity
>
> *Find out more about the* Common Core Principles for Working with Carers and Carers Matter – Everybody's Business *by downloading them from* www.skillsforcare.org.uk
>
> *Work through the eight principles and think about your current work and contact with family members, identify which principle you are most able to influence in practice and how.*

All equal, all different

As a paid worker with people with autism or people with a learning disability you will meet and work with a wide range of people and their family members. Learning disability and autism have no boundaries in terms of gender, class or culture and every person and every family member is unique. By the time you find yourself working with someone they will already have had years of life experiences. Their family's good and bad experiences of working with professionals may affect their attitude to working with you. It is important to understand the uniqueness of each person and to respect who they are as well as their family, culture and background. It is only in getting to know each other that trust and respect for each other can grow – even if you do not always agree.

Acknowledging that partnership with family members is the way of working means agreeing from the start:

- how the partnership will work in practice;
- how everyone will know that partnership working is happening and is working well;
- how it will be reviewed;
- how successes will be recorded;
- how any difficulties will be resolved.

Paid staff working with experts

You will do your job in partnership with a range of people who bring specialist knowledge. Family carers will have become expert in understanding and supporting their son or daughter or sibling and should always be respected as equal partners with paid staff in supporting their relative. Family members, especially parents, will have years of knowledge and understanding about how their relative likes to be supported – what makes them happy and fulfilled and what makes them sad, angry or frustrated; how they communicate their wants, needs and emotions; how they like to spend their leisure time; who they like to spend time with and so much more. Family usually remains important to all of us – remember that the person you support may be a brother, sister, cousin, uncle or aunt. These roles and relationships continue, members of the family will carry on being interested in each other's wellbeing.

Being aware of the person's roles and tapping into their expert experience and knowledge can make your job easier and give the person a better quality of life. Provided it is what the person you support wants, you should also be enabling their relatives to continue to be involved in agreed and chosen ways. Working in inclusive and respectful ways will help your relationship with family members to be positive and rewarding.

> **Activity**
>
> *Think of three actions you could take to ensure that the family members that you know are valued and appreciated? How can you make and maintain a good relationship with family members? Discuss your ideas with one of the family members, if this is appropriate. Alternatively, discuss it with your line manager at your next supervision.*

A good relationship has a pattern like a dance and is built on some of the same rules. The partners do not need to hold on tightly, because they move confidently in the same pattern, intricate but gay and swift and free, like a country dance of Mozart's. To touch heavily would be to arrest the pattern and freeze the movement, to check the endlessly changing beauty of its unfolding. There is no place here for the possessive clutch, the clinging arm, the heavy hand; only the barest touch in passing. Now arm in arm, now face to face, now back to back – it does not matter which. Because they know they are partners moving to the same rhythm, creating a pattern together, and being invisibly nourished by it.

Anne Morrow Lindbergh

> **Thinking point**
>
> *What can we learn about partnership working with family members from this description of a good relationship?*

Paid staff and family members will usually share a wish to support the person to be a valued member of their community and to have the control to live the life they choose with the support they need. This means respecting the needs and wishes of the person, and this includes how much involvement they wish to have with their family. You will be an important link between the person and their family which will be more effective if you can establish a good working relationship and partnership with the family.

Valuing families

For most of us, our families provide love, support and shared times. It is often with our parents, siblings or other close relatives that we share a whole range of family experiences, memories and a sense of identity in our local community. Our relatives may be our most honest critics. Family relationships help to make us who we are and this is no different for the families of people with learning disabilities and people with autism.

In the past, parents were sometimes seen as awkward and difficult, especially when their preferred way forward differed from that of paid workers. When this happened paid staff found it is easier to ignore the family's experience and knowledge, seeing them as interfering if they remain involved in the relative's life after they leave the parental home.

Thinking point

How often are you in touch with your family? How does your family celebrate special occasions such as birthdays, holidays or festivals? What family times do you share that are special for you? Is it any different for the people you support?

As we have already seen, current government policies value families highly, respecting their expertise and their lifelong commitment and involvement in their relative's life, even when they have left the family home. In fact, this simply reflects how most people want to continue to remain in touch and spend time with their families, even when they have moved out of the parental home. The amount of contact will vary from individual to individual.

You will be in a unique position to help families strike a balance between the person's needs and wishes and their own. Even when they have left home, some people you support may continue to make considerable demand on their family. This could be at a time when older family members may themselves need care and support or, after years of caring, may wish to follow their own interests and friendships whilst they are able to. It is often a fine balance to meet everyone's needs and wishes.

Personalisation and self directed support

In recent years there have been major changes to the way social care is provided. Most of the big day centres have closed; large residential homes have gone to be replaced by smaller, more personalised settings. Direct payments and personal budgets have enabled people to develop individual ways of getting support. *Valuing People Now* (DH, 2009) was based on the values of rights, independence, choice and inclusion. It focused on people and their families having a voice and being at the centre of any plans for their support. This has led to many people with a learning disability getting more control over their own lives with the right support to do this. This is leading to a significant change in the role of paid staff.

The policies for developing more person centred, individualised support known as 'personalisation' means starting with the person and their individual needs and wishes rather than simply trying to fit someone into an available service. It is essential that as a paid worker you really understand what this means for the people that you support and for yourself as a worker. It is a fundamentally different way of relating to the people that you support. It is about stepping back and giving people the time to say what they want. Your focus should be on actively listening and respecting people as fellow citizens rather than seeing them as service users. It is about enabling people to have choice and control in day to day decisions – such as what to eat, wear or do – and bigger decisions such as where they want to live and who with, if anyone else. You can find out more about personalisation in the book *Personalisation: A Rough Guide* (2011) from www.scie.org.uk

A key part of personalisation is the planning process that includes identifying who will provide any support that is needed. This could be paid staff (employed by an organisation), personal assistants (employed directly by the person themselves, or their family, or a trust), family or friends. Such planning could include a 'circle of support', which is a group of people who know the person well, love and care about them, and who meet to help them plan and make changes in their life. Circles of support tackle a range of issues such as finding people the individual can go to the cinema with or working through major changes such as moving house. You can find out more information about circles of support from Circles Network on circlesnetwork.org.uk

More people with autism and people with a learning disability are now choosing self directed support as a way of organising the support they need through a personal budget or direct payments, and the expectation is that this will increase. This means that as a paid worker you may have a very different relationship with a family member – they may be your employer, on behalf of a son or daughter, for example, or you may be employed by the person you are supporting.

> Since Joe has been employing his own personal assistants and being in control of his own life there's been a big difference in his speech – he's using more words and enjoys having conversations more. People are giving him time, talking with him calmly and clearly without using metaphors. As a family we have trained Joe's personal assistants to be Joe-centred in the way they work with him. Every morning Joe does a plan for the day – it gives him and his PAs a great structure for the day and puts him in the driving seat.
>
> *Chris, Joe's mum*

Having a positive relationship with a person's family will help everyone and also improve the quality of life of the person you work with.

Thinking point

Think about your current work setting, how will your work change as people with autism and people with a learning disability have more choice and control over their lives and how they are supported. What do you think their family's role in this might be?

Key points from this chapter

- Families frequently play a very important role in the lives of people with a learning disability and people with autism. They often have considerable knowledge and understanding of their relative and how they communicate their needs and wishes.

- Recent government policies value the expertise and knowledge that families have, recognising that they are experts and emphasising the importance of partnership working.

- The key values on which partnership working with family carers is based include respecting the uniqueness of each person and their family; integrity, listening to and hearing what people and their families have to say and responding positively.

- Agreeing to work in partnership with family members means agreeing with them how this will work in practice from the start.

- Respecting family members as equal partners can help you to support people with a learning disability and people with autism more effectively.

- Support workers are an important link between the person and their family. This will be most effective if you can establish a good working relationship and partnership with family members.

- The new policies on personalisation and self directed support give disabled people, and their families, more of a voice; they place them at the centre of any plans for their support. The goal is for people with a learning disability and people with autism to get more control over their own lives, with the right support to do this. This will lead to significant changes in the future role of paid staff.

References and where to go for more information

References

Mencap (2007) *Death by Indifference.* London: Mencap

Morrow Lindbergh, A (1955) *Gifts from the Sea.* New York: Pantheon

SCIE (2011) *Personalisation: A rough guide.* London:SCIE. Downloadable from www.scie.org.uk

Skills for Care (2011) *Carers Matter – Everybody's Business.* Downloadable from www.skillsforcare.org.uk

Skills for Health (2011) *Common Core Principles for Working with Family Carers.* Downloadable from www.skillsforhealth.org.uk

Legislation, policies and reports

Department of Health (2008) *Healthcare for All: The report of the independent inquiry into access to healthcare for people with learning disabilities – Sir Jonathan Michael*. London: Department of Health. Downloadable from www.dh.gov.uk

Policies and legislation for England can be downloaded from www.dh.gov.uk

Policies and legislation for Northern Ireland can be downloaded from www.dhsspsni.gov.uk

Policies and legislation for Scotland can be downloaded from www.scotland.gov.uk

Policies and legislation for Wales can be downloaded from www.wales.gov.uk

Websites

Hft Family Carer Support Services www.hft.org.uk

In Control www.in-control.org.uk

National Autistic Society www.nas.org.uk

National Family Carer Network www.familycarers.org.uk

SCIE www.scie.org.uk

Think Local Act Personal www.thinklocalactpersonal.org.uk

Chapter 2
Understanding partnership working with families

Paul's Story

We knew that leaving home for our son, Paul, was always going to be a wrench. New situations, change of any kind had always been a challenge needing careful planning and preparation to ease his acute anxiety. But at age 19 he had decided that he would like to go to residential college. Several visits to the college had made the experience more appealing – working on the college farm, looking after pigs, living with a young family.

But the most helpful part of the preparation was that staff at the college acknowledged the difficulties and talked with us, his family, about them. It was they who suggested several day visits in advance of the move. And they who suggested that when Paul moved in, it might help if I spent the first few nights there too. Their approach was respectful, flexible and most importantly it helped Paul to make the move from home in as easy a way possible.

Paul's mum

Introduction

Partnership working entails getting to know things about your partners so this chapter helps you to think about the significance of a person's family in their life. Every person and family is unique and families (including parents, grandparents, brothers and sisters, aunts and uncles, nieces and nephews) are likely to be of great importance to the people you support. You have a chance to think about the contribution families make both directly to the person and in terms of passing on their knowledge and expertise to you about how the person likes and needs to be supported. The chapter considers why not all families will be in a position to have active involvement in their relative's support but how their views should nevertheless be respected.

This chapter helps you to think about how to deal with differing opinions. It is important to be able to see things from another person's point of view and to recognise different perspectives and positions. The attitude of workers can make or break partnership working with families. Respect for families is essential in building up trust between paid staff and family members. Families have so much to offer if their involvement is supported in positive ways.

Learning outcomes

This chapter will help you to:

- analyse the contribution of families to the care and/or support of individuals;
- identify the factors that may affect the level of involvement of family members in care and/or support;
- describe the dilemmas or conflicts that may arise when working in partnership with families to support individuals;
- explain how the attitudes of a worker affect partnership working with families.

This chapter covers:

- Level 3 HSC 3038 – Work in partnership with families to support individuals: Learning Outcome 1

Understand the contribution of families to the care and support of individuals

> Like anyone who has tried to protect the integrity of a loved one with a chronic condition, my life with Nicholas has been infused by a desperate love. I have never met a parent of a disabled child who saw their child as 'tragic' – such children are adored for being their essential selves. What matters to Nicholas is to lead a life that is full, interesting and exciting in his terms and what has mattered to me is to be able to help him do that.
>
> *Donna Thomson*

Thinking point

Before you read on, make a list of what you think families contribute towards the care and support of their relative?

Early years

First and foremost, the contribution of parents to a disabled child is no different to that for any other child in terms of love, care and nurturing. However, right from the start when families first suspect or are told that their son or daughter has a disability, they will have had to cope with contact with a number of professionals that could include paediatricians, speech and language therapists, physiotherapists, occupational therapists, audiologists or, pre-school teachers amongst others.

If the child has any developmental delay, then therapists will have worked with the family to encourage play and learning. Each successful achievement will have been celebrated – an apparently small step forward giving enormous pleasure. At this early stage, parents will be doing much to support their child's development and they are likely to have paid staff working alongside them. The nature of these early relationships with professionals is likely to affect the way the family works with others later on.

During the childhood years of their son or daughter, the family will have developed expertise in both providing support and juggling the needs of other family members and themselves. This will result in many years of working with services, professionals and paid staff in a range of settings. By the time the young person leaves school and moves from children's to adult services, they and their family may have had contact with up to a hundred professionals or more and have developed skills in discerning who works well with them and their relative. Paid workers come and go – families are for life, and remember good and poor experiences.

During the individual's early years and adolescence the family contribution to the support of their relative will change but is likely to include:

- love;

- personal care;

- time and energy;

- learning about and dealing with health and social care systems and the benefits system;

- making choices and decisions on behalf of their son or daughter, beyond those for non-disabled children;

- knowledge and expertise related to any condition or syndrome;

The contribution of parents to the upbringing of a disabled child is no different to that of any other child in terms of love, care and nurturing.

- practical and emotional support (eg in socialising);
- advocacy;
- finding out about possible future options and how to achieve them;
- communication between the person and paid staff.

Love is what drives any parent to care for and nurture their young person. It is what binds families to each other. The demands of caring for a disabled young person are far greater than for a non-disabled child, but for many families the additional demands of caring for a disabled child frequently seem linked with a raised strength of feeling and commitment to do what is needed.

The continuing supporting role

The people you are supporting may still live with their family, be about to leave home for the first time or may have been living away from the family home for a long time. When a person does leave the family home to live more independently, it is unlikely that the family's relationship and support for their relative will stop. Over time the nature and level of support that is needed is likely to change, but the relationship between the person and their family will continue. When you are getting to know a person, the family's knowledge and experience can be invaluable to paid staff. Close relatives can help things to go well and problem solve when they do not.

Unfortunately the culture in many services and settings still does not always encourage family carer involvement. This is a loss for everyone concerned and especially the person being supported. When families feel they are being excluded or not listened to they are likely to question why staff are defensive towards them – is there abuse of some kind happening, are they too busy to treat their relative as an individual, do they not really care enough about the people they work with? Individually and in groups, family members, motivated by their strong sense of commitment to their relatives have publicised cases of harm and injustice and been effective in lobbying for change. They monitor quality of care and support in the way you are likely to do if you have a relative who is dependent on paid staff!

If there is a strong relationship between the person and their family, then obviously their family will be very important to them.

The person's family is likely to be a significant part of their life – just like any other family, they are often their rock. And because families know the person so well and have many years' experience of supporting them, they can be a huge resource to paid workers.

Of course people reach a point where they want to make their own choices and decisions – it's the same for all sons and daughters growing up. And it's important to understand how it must feel for families – there is still a need for support and it must be hard to see someone else take on that role. You have to be very sensitive.

Sarah Holdstock, Support Worker

The family of a person you support are likely to be a significant part of their life – just like any other family.

Involvement in planning

In this short paragraph, taken from the book *An Introduction to Supporting People with Autistic Spectrum Conditions* (2011) Joe's mum reveals so much and gives us many things to consider in learning about Joe. Notice how important the drink of cola is. It is the motivator for Joe and has been used

> Joe has always liked his drinks of cola. He also likes pictures of cola bottles and cans and photos of different members of the family drinking cola themselves. We used to have an album with photos of each of us drinking from a can or a bottle of cola. Joe would laugh and point to each of us and the cola. Joe also went horse riding at the local riding for the disabled club and he enjoyed swimming, but not in the public pool – just too many people around. We found a family near us who have their own pool and they let us use it twice a week when Joe was at home. Of course you always had to have a drink of cola after being riding or swimming but he did enjoy both activities.
>
> *Joe's mum*

by his family brilliantly – to engage with him, to make him laugh and to get him out and enjoying physical activities like swimming. The drink of cola is a predictable and much loved factor in Joe's life and it has been used cleverly to support Joe to explore new experiences and make these experiences feel safe.

Because families have so much knowledge and experience to share they can contribute both to initial support planning and to the development of a person centred care plan. They will probably have been thinking in a person centred way about their relative for years and so have lots to contribute to the support plan. Their understanding of the person's individuality, their self esteem, how they like to be supported, what makes them happy, their abilities and skills can all enrich the planning. Although they may not have used the 'tools' and recording systems that paid staff are familiar with, they will be used to assessing and working with their relative's capacity to understand options and make choices, thinking about risks and dealing with the consequences of decisions. They will have a view about what support is needed and know how their relative prefers their support to be provided. In addition, they will be aware of the importance of communicating clearly with other supporters or partners in care, in cases of unexpected changes to routine, ill-health, anticipation, excitement, fear or dislike of someone or something.

As a paid worker your views and the words that you use may be different from a relative's. It is important not to use jargon that families may not be familiar with. A non-judgemental approach is vital as you learn about a person's and their family's values and lifestyles.

If the person and their family have different perspectives and goals, you will need to understand and work towards agreeing a shared way forward together. Is there information that either the person needing support or their relative does not yet have that could help them find a way forward? For example – does the person who says they do not want to tell their family about a trip they have chosen to go on understand this may hurt their feelings and be discovered in due course anyway? Why would they like to keep it a secret – can you help with anything that worries them about telling their family? Does their family – who you know likes information about future plans – understand what a big step it was for the person to make this choice themselves and about the support they have had to weigh up the pros and cons before making up their own mind about when to tell the family about it?

Each person with a learning disability and person with autism should be involved in developing their support plan so that it reflects the support that they need, how this will be given and by whom. When someone lacks the capacity to understand a specific choice, any decision or action must be taken in their best interests and follow the procedures relating to the mental capacity legislation for the country in which they live. Making a 'best interests' decision does not mean choosing what to do 'for the best' on someone else's behalf; instead those who know the person well should have the opportunity to share what they believe the person would choose if they were able to in making the decision. Family carers should be supported to know about the Mental Capacity Act and how they can help the Act work well for their relative. In England and Wales it is a legal requirement of the Mental Capacity Act (2005) that family members are consulted in circumstances when a person lacks capacity to make a particular decision. In Scotland, people need to work to the requirements set out in the Adults with Incapacity Act (Scotland) 2000 and in Northern Ireland mental capacity issues are currently dealt with under common law although there are plans to introduce mental capacity legislation.

Activity

Find out from your manager about the arrangements in your organisation for supporting people with decision making and for assessing capacity. Also find out how family members are involved and have access to information so that they can be partners in making 'best interest' decisions.

Ongoing support through advice

Remember that relatives are likely to be able to offer relevant advice when new situations arise. The contribution of a family member through a five minute telephone call could help resolve a potentially difficult situation or provide the information required to ensure that new opportunities are appropriate and available.

Formal family support

Some families support their relative to draw up their support plan and assist them to organise and manage their support, by employing personal assistants on their behalf or through an independent living trust.

The factors that may affect the level of involvement of family members in support

Most families of people with a learning disability and people with autism will have cared for their son or daughter at home during their childhood, adolescent and early adult years. This may have meant years of 24 hours a day caring and sleepless nights, together with endless negotiations with education, health and social services. Many families talk about having to 'fight' for the support that they know their son or daughter needs. All of this can be exhausting. It may also mean that family members miss out on ordinary life opportunities because they are always caring or supporting. In addition family members worry about the future when they will not be able to do what they currently do to look out for their relative.

One family describes how they feel about having to fight for services:

> I don't feel 'why me?' – after all – 'why not?' – but more a sense that other people, including service providers, lack a perception of what caring is all about. When this happens I find myself wishing yet again that it hadn't happened to our family.
>
> *Mother of a young man with Down's syndrome*

For some families, it is their disabled child who keeps them going. Family members say that caring about a disabled relative is a strong motivator. Paula's mum says:

> Paula has such a strong extrovert personality – it forces people to see her as a person rather than just seeing her disability. It makes it easier for us to cope too – she's a great help to us in that way.
>
> *Paula's mum*

When a person with autism or a person with a learning disability leaves the family home they do not leave the family. It is only natural that their family will want to keep a close eye on their well being and the quality of support they are receiving in the short and longer term. Family members want to know that others can provide good, reliable support that helps their relative develop their interests and skills and to have confidence they will have a safe and fulfilled life without them being ever-present. Their wish for this can make relatives seem over anxious or critical. Previous poor practice may have added to this. Separations will have already happened through their relative going to nursery, school, college, day time or holiday activities with friends or using short breaks services – and there may have been disappointments with unpleasant consequences when things have not gone well. You have the opportunity to prove other people can give good support.

Be careful not to make any assumptions about a family member being able or wanting to continue all aspects of their caring role on the basis of family relationships, cultural stereotypes or previous history.

Family members may be wanting to adjust their role because they:

- are exhausted from 20, 30 or 40 years of caring;
- are older carers;
- have their own health issues which limit their ability to continue to care;
- are supporting other relatives or friends or have other family commitments;
- have difficulty visiting because of the distance or a lack of transport;

- want to have a life beyond caring – for example, having a job and a social life that is not centred on disability;

- are dealing with illness, family crisis, bereavement, redundancy or any of life's daily stresses.

This may mean that other family members become more involved in the life of the person you support; if so, you will have a role to play in sensitively enabling this.

Moving on

As we have explained above, family members may have conflicting feelings about other people supporting their relative. If you work in a residential or supported living setting, you may meet family members who find it difficult to adjust when their relative leaves home – this is not unique to families of people with autism or people with a learning disability. However welcome it might be, they will be giving up their day to day caring role, they may feel they are suddenly excluded from a son or daughter's life. They may feel empty, find it difficult to re-establish such a meaningful role in their life and be struggling to cope with the extra time that they have. It may be difficult for them to see where they fit into their son or daughter's life now.

You could equally be working with people who have been living away from their families for many years, where family involvement may be limited to reviews and occasional visits. Some people may have no family members in their lives. Whatever factors are affecting how family carers engage with the person you support, you will need to treat them in the same person centred way that you would like to be treated

Family members can find it difficult to adjust when their relative leaves home to move into a place of their own.

– with sensitivity, respect, empathy and recognition that circumstances and feelings change.

Nothing as certain as change

Change is one thing that is inevitable for all of us in our lives. Even positive changes such as getting a new job, meeting a new partner or moving into a new flat or house can be extremely challenging. For people with a learning disability or with autism, change is often one of the hardest things they have to cope with. In particular for people with autism, predictability and consistency are usually very important to them. People with autism may resent, resist and become very distressed at change or loss, especially if it is sudden. Major life events such as bereavement or moving home can be traumatic for them, but even a small change, such as a different coloured taxi into town may cause serious anxiety and distress. Working together to anticipate and overcome difficulties is therefore essential.

When faced with supporting someone with planned or unplanned changes, it is important that shared approaches can be developed through an ongoing, frank and open dialogue between you and the family. This way everyone can decide together, with the person, how best to meet their changing needs and wishes in a positive, holistic way and how any difficulties can be addressed in partnership. Working in this way will also ensure that the needs of family members, and the family as a whole, can be identified and addressed.

The dilemmas or conflicts that may arise when working in partnership with families to support individuals

Unique models of the world

> It's important to have empathy – you have to get to understand the worker's situation as much as they have to understand ours. Both sides need to put themselves in the other person's shoes.
>
> *Frank, Angie's dad*

Many people assume that everyone else experiences the world in the same way that they do. Such assumptions can lead to a clash of expectations, disappointment and friction that may last if not handled well. It is important to remember we all experience and respond to the world differently, creating our own 'model of the world' as we go along. Our experiences and our response to them make us who we are. Being aware that we are working with other people's personal model helps us to realise that their world is no more right or wrong than ours.

> **Thinking point**
>
> *If you played the same song to ten different people would they all like it? Would they all describe it in the same way?*

Recognising different values and views will not only enable you to support a person through working with an understanding of their view of the world, it will also assist you to avoid conflict and deal with dilemmas as they arise.

> As we grow as unique persons, we learn to respect the uniqueness of others.
>
> *Robert H Schuller*

> You will come across:
>
> - Different view points
>
> You and a family member may have different views about what activities the person you support takes part in, who they spend time with or how they should be supported. It may even seem the family member is never satisfied and their demands are affecting how others are being supported. Emotions can run high, anger and frustration making it difficult to negotiate a way forward unless you have established a good relationship with the family member. Recognising that they are working with positive intentions, from their unique model of the world (which may include poor practice in the past) is a good starting point and vital to maintain rapport and avoid standoffs. Your employer or manager has a responsibility to support you in this situation.

> - Family members may disagree amongst themselves about how the person is supported
>
> This can create a complex dilemma for you as you have to deal with different people's perspectives on how you provide support. The need to establish partnership and collaboration is important in these situations; listening to and understanding different viewpoints without giving an opinion can be a helpful first step. Again you should not deal with this alone but discuss it with your employer – even if this is the family whose views are not consistent – or your manager.

You will not be expected to facilitate family relationships on your own and you may have to make this clear to the people involved. Your employer or manager has a responsibility to support you with this. Sometimes varying opinions can be resolved by explaining how the capacity legislation works (as above) or by going back to the support plan – does this say what was agreed about the issue? Who was involved in support planning with the person and was informed agreement given?

If there are disagreements about how decisions have been taken about support for a person, family members have every right to ask how the decision was made. If they are not already familiar with the Mental Capacity Act, or the relevant mental capacity legislation for the country they are in, it will be helpful to explain to family members how the legislation says decisions should be made. Provided they have capacity to make a particular decision the Act says adults should do so, with any support they need. You may need to describe how someone's capacity to make a decision was assessed and how support was given.

If a person does not have capacity they should be supported to be as involved in the decision as possible but a best interest process should be followed. Relatives should be involved if a formal best interests meeting occurs, but even if it is not they are likely to have ideas about the best ways of providing relevant information and understanding their communication.

It's easy to feel defensive if your decisions are being challenged but a positive outcome is more likely if you discuss family members' genuine concerns openly and avoid being defensive. They may have relevant information that affects a person's choices or risk management plans or someone else's duty of care.

It is important that you have the opportunity to receive supervision and support from your line manager who should provide opportunities to talk about the issues constructively.

There may be times when you face different and competing demands on your time and the way you work, especially as you may be supporting several people at the same time. Demands from other people you support and family members, together with the pressures of working to a rota may lead to conflict. Your organisation will have policies in place that will set out some of the things you need to do, and you may need to be guided by your line manager as to the priorities you need to follow. It is important to be open and honest about any difficulties and share these with colleagues and in particular your line manager in supervision, to find solutions.

Tracey's story

Tracey feared that being on the contraceptive pill may not be safe for her daughter, Lisa, and mentioned this regularly because of her anxiety and knowledge that 'there was cancer in the family'. Staff were aware of the mother's concern but also respected that Lisa's informed choice was to use the pill; they explained to Tracey that their role was to support Lisa's ability and right to make this choice. When Lisa's cousin learnt of new research evidence about risks associated with the long term use of the particular pill that Lisa was taking, the family asked that she be given the new information and a chance to consider alternative contraception in future. The information they provided was taken seriously and Lisa was again supported to make a decision for herself.

You may wish to impose your model of the world on to the person you support as you have an interest in something you are so enthusiastic about that you want to share it with everyone. However, when supporting someone with a learning disability or with autism it's important that the starting point is their model of the world. You need to support them to find their own particular interests. This will involve active listening in giving the person time to express their wishes and helping them to explore new opportunities.

This does not mean that you do not share your interests with each other – this is a natural thing to do. Some people and organisations take a person centred approach to employing support workers, matching you with the person's own unique model of the world based on your personality and interests. In this situation shared passions and interests can be positively encouraged.

But ultimately it is their model of the world that counts. As a paid worker you may be privileged to be told memories or stories from the people that you work with about their private family life including some that other people would probably not talk about. Remember that this is private and confidential information. It is important to be respectful and maintain confidentiality about such stories which may be complex and highly sensitive while at the same time knowing when to share anything you have concerns about with your supervisor.

> **Thinking point**
>
> *Thinking about your own family, are there memories, stories and incidents that you would not want to be spoken about openly to others?*

Supporting the person

Your primary responsibility will always be to the person you are supporting to get to understand their likes, dislikes, their possibilities and desires, and to support them to have a life that they enjoy and find fulfilling.

Most relatives of people with autism or with a learning disability take great pride in what their family member has achieved. But remember their family's model of the world is likely to have been shaped by the experiences of having to engage with the systems set up to help them, such as assessments, reviews, numerous meetings with professionals and applications for benefits or personal budgets, which all represent intrusion, pressure, anxiety and fatigue that most other families do not have to cope with. The constant changes in the systems and social care models with reorganisations and new staff members are all part of a system of support over which families and people with a learning disability and people with autism have little or no control.

A family's model of the world will also be shaped in part by their experience of the discrimination and exclusion that disabled people and their families may face, sometimes with a lack of recognition for their efforts in doing their best for their son, daughter or sibling. Their model of the world will also be underpinned by a lifelong relationship of close trust and love and with a desire to get the best available support to enhance their relative's life.

Activity

Multiple perspectives: A way to get a better understanding of a family's unique model of the world

This activity will help you to think more creatively and flexibly about your partnership with family members and other partners. It will give you a better understanding of the family member's situation and provide an opportunity to consider the important issues in an objective way. In addition, it will give you an insight into how your attitudes and behaviour can affect other people and likewise how their behaviour can influence and have an impact on you.

You can use this to think about a past situation or to plan ahead for one in the future.

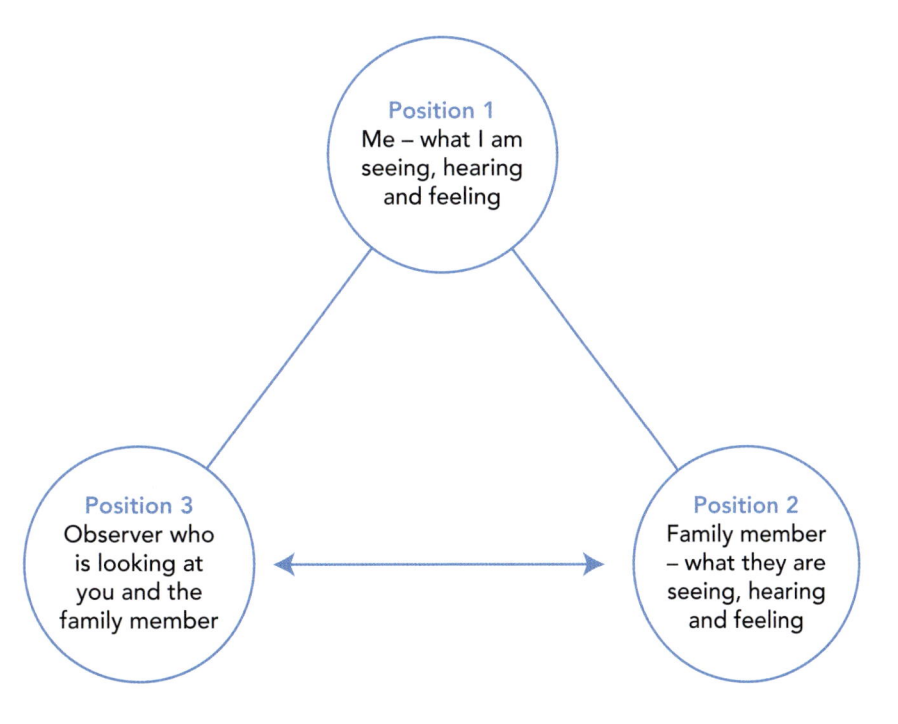

Position 1
Me – what I am seeing, hearing and feeling

Position 3
Observer who is looking at you and the family member

Position 2
Family member – what they are seeing, hearing and feeling

This is an activity that is best to do with another person.

One person does the exercise. The other coaches the person through the exercise by giving guidance and receiving feedback from any questions.

Think about a recent interaction that you have had with a family member which made you feel uncomfortable or where the conversation did not turn out the way that you anticipated.

Mark out three different places on the floor (as in the diagram above). You can walk into each position as you work through the activity. Or you could set out three chairs and move to each chair to take on each different position.

There are two stages to this exercise.

Stage 1

Position 1
Think about the recent interaction through your own eyes: become aware of your thoughts and how you are feeling. Notice your body posture and your needs when thinking through the interaction.

- What is important to you in this situation?
- Are you getting the outcome that you wanted?
- What do you feel about the other person?

Position 2
Move into this position and imagine what it is like to be the other person, really taking on their persona. When you talk, talk in the first person using the word 'I' rather than the person's name. For example, you would say 'I was worried' rather than 'Mrs Smith was worried'.

Put yourself in their shoes – seeing, feeling and hearing what they are experiencing looking back at you – and notice.

- How does the person in position 1 seem to you?
- Do they understand you and your point of view?
- What do you think about them?
- What is really important to you in this situation and is this being recognised?
- What do you feel about this?

Position 3
Move into the third position and take a detached, objective viewpoint. Imagine you are looking at the family member in position 2 and yourself in position 1.

- What is their body language revealing?
- What is the tone of their voices?
- What communication is taking place – is there rapport and understanding?

> From this viewpoint, think about what advice you would like to give yourself about how you are handling the situation.
>
> - What would need to happen to improve things?
> - What have you learnt and what would you do differently?
> - Could the outcome have been different?
>
> **Stage 2**
>
> Now repeat the process from the beginning, using what you have learnt from the exercise so far. Adopt a new approach, firstly as yourself, then as the family member in the second position and thirdly as the detached view point.
>
> This exercise is adapted from the Neuro-linguistic Programming (NLP) technique 'Perceptual Positions'. For more information on NLP visit http://nlpuniversitypress.com/

How the attitudes of a worker can affect partnership working with families

> My most vivid memory of great help from a paid worker happened more than 30 years ago – they say people never forget a good teacher! My son's pre-school peripatetic teacher was a real inspiration. She treated me as an equal and worked alongside us as a family, encouraging and advising, but never judging. She saw her role as an enabler, but she was more than that. She thought holistically about all our family's needs. She encouraged us to apply for benefits no one else had told us about and she encouraged me to do something for myself beyond my role as a parent. She went the extra mile and that made all the difference.
>
> *Parent of a 35 year old man with learning disabilities and autism*

If you respect the experience and expertise of family members whose relatives you support, then you will be willing to accept and value them for the people they are. As paid staff, it is important to actively welcome the contribution of families to the support of their relative. Remember that it is easy for family members to feel that they are expected to 'hand over' that responsibility. Let them know you expect to work in partnership with them and remember some families may need encouragement to continue to play a part in their relative's life.

> The way the service is provided and the attitudes of individual paid staff can have a significant effect on how families cope.
>
> I often feel angry and unvalued because I know the amount of energy and effort I've put in for years and years and years – but nobody seems to recognise that.
>
> Alison is the person she is because I've always challenged and encouraged her. She is still growing as an individual – which is a real achievement and I don't want that to stop. But she finds it difficult to articulate what she's interested in. You have to make suggestions – until she's tried something she doesn't know if she likes it or not. (These days in her service….) There's no forward planning with Alison about what she does, no proper communication. It's quite upsetting and demoralising.
>
> Most parents want to work with professionals. What needs to change is the adversarial, defensive context – the 'them and us' so there can be an honest, respectful two way dialogue.
>
> *Pauline Rogers, Alison's mum*

Activity

Think about what Pauline has said in this quote. How would you be supporting Alison in this situation? What would you be talking about to Pauline? How could you all work together to support Alison to get the life she chooses? Discuss your ideas with your line manager or a senior colleague.

In the past there has often been a power imbalance with paid staff being seen as in control of how a person was supported. However, this is likely to change as the impact of the carers' strategy is felt and as more people with a learning disability and autism choose to direct their own support and employ their own personal assistants or paid staff. Within these new relationships paid staff will be directly answerable to individuals and their families who will be responsible for training and supervising paid workers.

Within these new relationships, families and paid staff should be able to work together as allies of the person they are supporting. However, it is only when families really trust paid staff that the partnership is likely to work well.

Individuals and those closest to them will be looking for personal assistants who are eager to respect and work with them in delivering person centred support. They will want personal assistants who have great ideas for involving their relative as a citizen in their community.

Enabling the person to develop new relationships, and build on existing connections within their community is likely to be an important part of the job. Your attitude to this will make the difference to its success or otherwise. You will need to be able to introduce the person to people within their community with the appropriate level of support and direction. The family is likely to be a valuable resource for building networks and links in the local community especially if they have lived in the area for a long time. You will need to be able to work together constructively with the person and their family to meet their needs and help achieve their wishes.

Supporting a person leaving the family home

Earlier in this chapter we have mentioned some issues that may arise for family members when a relative moves on from their family home. For people on the autistic spectrum, a major change in their lives such as this can be especially stressful. In these situations, family members are an essential resource of information for getting to know someone new to you, especially if they do not use speech. You can find out from family members about the person's particular interests, things that fascinate them and how they can be supported to cope with change.

> **Thinking point**
>
> *What questions might you want to ask the family members of someone with autism that you are just starting to work with? How would you begin to get to know the person? How would you try to understand how their autism affects their life?*

When their relative leaves home is likely to be a stressful time for the family and the individual too. There are particular things you can do to help them both. Having as much information as possible about the person from their family members will help you to support them to settle comfortably into their new life. Excellent communication and passing on any relevant information will be crucial at this time and can set the pattern for a good working relationship between paid staff and families in the future. It is very important that families feel that they are being 'kept in the loop' even if this means having to be honest but sensitive about any difficulties.

> **Thinking point**
>
> *What habits of a close relative of yours such as a brother, sister, son or daughter would you know about that would take other people time to learn?*

Key points from this chapter

- Being respectful of people's family experiences for both the people that you support and their family members is essential to supporting someone well.
- Families are likely to be a person's lifelong supporters and will have vital expertise and experience of how their relative likes to be supported.
- Families will have a valuable role to play in planning with their relative and in monitoring the support they receive and whether they are living a happy and fulfilling life.
- You will need to have an accepting, positive, empathetic, respectful and encouraging attitude for good partnership working.
- The future level of involvement of family members will depend on many things including their own work or health situation or indeed whether the person chooses them to be involved.
- Everyone has their own unique model of the world. How family members see the world will have been shaped by their experiences of the health and social care system.
- The mental capacity legislation for the country that you work in should direct you in resolving differences of opinion on choice and decision making.

References and where to go for more information

References

Cowen, A (2002) *Taking Care.* York: Joseph Rowntree Foundation
http://www.jrf.org.uk

Hatton, S and Boughton, T (2011) *An Introduction to Supporting People with Autistic Spectrum Conditions.* Exeter: Learning Matters/BILD

Thomson, D (2010) *The Four Walls of My Freedom.* McArthur and Company
www.donnathomson.blogspot.com

Hft's Family Carer Support Service (2011) *Using the Mental Capacity Act: A Resource for Families and Friends of People with Learning Disabilities.* Downloadable from: http://bit.ly/raonaY

National Family Carer Network and Hft (2012) *Making sure your Relative is Safe. Top Tips for Family Carers about 'Safeguarding' Adults with Learning Disabilities.* Downloadable from: www.hft.org.uk/safeguarding

Schuller, R, quote from: www.simplyaninspiredlife.com

Legislation, policies and reports

All UK legislation can be downloaded from www.legislation.gov.uk

Policies and reports for Northern Ireland, Scotland and Wales can be found at www.northernireland.gov.uk, www.scotland.gov.uk and www.wales.gov.uk respectively. Policies and reports for England can be found on the website of the relevant government department.

Mental Capacity Act (2005) – applies to England and Wales

Adults with Incapacity (Scotland) Act (2000)

Northern Ireland currently does not have mental capacity legislation. Mental capacity issues are dealt with under common law. Mental capacity legislation is likely to be introduced in 2014.

Websites

Carers UK www.carersuk.com

Circles Network www.circlesnetwork.org.uk

HFT Family Carer Support Services www.hft.org.uk

National Family Carer Network www.familycarers.org.uk

Chapter 3

Establishing and maintaining positive relationships with families

> Angie's family designed and created the support for their daughter using direct payments. Frank and Judi say:
>
> When we did the training for the original set of workers we explained about our negative experiences with other staff and that this is what we didn't want to happen.
>
> Apart from a couple of niggles, we have no complaints and I think that shows a good partnership between staff and us. The partnership we created has become more organic – it's not a set structure, it's flexible. And the staff demonstrate openly that they care about Angie.

Introduction

This chapter will allow you to think about how to build good working relationships with family members which then means that everyone is clear about their role in supporting the person as effectively as possible.

To achieve this, you will need to get to know people well, respecting their unique view of the world, their background, their culture and religion, and their many years of experience and expertise and their ongoing interest in supporting their relative.

To gain the respect of family members, you will need to be sure that you always deliver what you say that you will do. You may not always agree with family members so this chapter identifies ways of resolving or working round any difficulties or conflict with families.

> **Learning Outcomes**
>
> This chapter will help you to:
>
> - establish and maintain positive relationships with families;
> - interact with family members in ways that respect their culture, experiences and expertise;
> - demonstrate dependability in carrying out the actions agreed with families;
> - describe the principles and ways of addressing dilemmas or conflicts that may arise in relationships with families.
>
> **This chapter covers:**
>
> Level 3 HSC 3038 – Work in partnership with families to support individuals: Learning Outcome 2

Establishing and maintaining positive relationships with families

A framework for working in inclusive and valuing ways can be remembered as the 4Rs. These are:

The 4Rs

Respect

Recognition

Reassurance

Rapport

1. Respect

Working with respect and a genuine interest for family members is essential. They will have supported and cared for their relative long before you enter their life and will continue to do so when you no longer work with them.

There is an old adage that: 'you have to earn respect'. It is reasonable that a relative who has supported and cared for their family member with autism or a learning disability into adulthood has earned the right to respect.

> Paid staff knowing our culture is important to me though I have no problem with them taking my brother to the pub as long as he does not have alcohol because for us that's bad.
>
> *Kausar Iqbal, sister and family carer to her two brothers with a learning disability*

One way of showing and earning respect can be by spending time listening to a family member's point of view. This creates opportunities for them to share their beliefs and values. Many family members may have struggled for years to have their views and opinions listened to by professionals and may have felt disrespected by not being valued or even acknowledged.

Other ways of showing respect are:

- taking time to get to know family members;

One way of showing respect can be by spending time listening to the person you support and to a family member's point of view.

- taking family members' feelings into consideration;
- ensuring that any meetings or reviews are arranged at a convenient time for family members and that they receive any written information in good time;
- making sure that regular communication takes place to share what is happening in their relative's life;
- understanding and valuing their past and present experience;
- asking family members for opinions and views on a regular basis;
- being welcoming and accepting;
- being open and honest without being defensive.

You can show respect for family members by creating an atmosphere where they can express their feelings and beliefs, where they are being listened to and taken seriously, and where they feel that they will be consulted when appropriate. Remember what usually makes you feel respected. This is likely to include you feeling that the atmosphere is safe for you to express your feelings and you feel listened to.

> As long as we have the photos of things that Edward likes and show them to him, so that he knows we will soon be home or the car is not very far away, he will calm down. Edward can understand the words but they don't help. The photos do. Using photos to support communication with Edward is essential.
>
> *Elizabeth, mum to Edward who has autism and doesn't use speech*

Thinking point

As a support worker meeting Edward and his family for the first time, what do you learn from this information from his mother, above? What actions will you take to help you get to know Edward and develop your relationship with him and his mother?

Avoid telling family members what to do, giving advice that is not asked for, insisting on telling them what they need, or ignoring the importance of their relationship with the person you support.

Some family members may well be better informed than you are about their relative's condition or about available services. You can seize on this as an opportunity to improve your own knowledge, and maybe find out things to pass on to other families or better still encourage family members to learn from each other. If family members appear to be uninformed, then you can empower them by passing on relevant information and the details of where they could get further information.

Some of the things family members might respect you for are:

- the way you relate to and support their relative;
- the way you relate and communicate with them;
- your willingness to listen and value their views and opinions;
- doing what you say you will do;
- the way you contact them on a regular basis to let them know about their relative;
- the way that you support their relative to contact them.

You might find two other books in this series helpful: *An Introduction to Supporting People with Autistic Spectrum Conditions* (2011) by Sue Hatton and Tom Boughton and *Next Steps in Supporting People with Autistic Spectrum Conditions* (2012) by Sue Hatton and John Simpson.

2. Recognition

Recognition is to acknowledge something. It seems such a simple concept but it is very important for us all. In particular, recognition is important for family members as their efforts in supporting their relative may go unrecognised at a hidden cost.

Even when it is some time since they have supported and cared day to day for a relative, the past and present contributions of family members should be fully recognised by paid staff. Not to do this would be a disrespectful failure to acknowledge their interest in the person, the skills, knowledge and experience that could be used to enhance the quality of the support provided to them.

Our first experience of a manager in the small group home my son moved to was fantastic. The atmosphere of the flat was welcoming and positive. She was genuinely pleased to meet Scott and us, his parents. She really listened to Scott and almost immediately they were having a great conversation about Scott's favourite bands. She had a genuine regard for me as his mum and truly wanted to hear my views and took them on board. Imagine our disappointment when this manager left only to be replaced by someone who was just the opposite – defensive and suspicious. We no longer felt welcome in our son's home; we found it difficult to discuss things that were important to us and our son. It felt very disempowering. When Scott became very unhappy we decided it was time for him to move on. A lesson in how one individual can make all the difference.

Parent of Scott, a young man with a learning disability and autism

You can maintain a positive relationship with families by recognising the family's journey, their relationship with the person you support, their love and positive intention and their religious and cultural practices.

Recognise the journey

The family member and the person that you support have been on a journey of experiences, some of which has been positive and some has been negative – in both cases a lot of learning has been gained. Recognising this journey not only respects the family member, but it also gives access to knowledge that can support you to support them. Get to know their journey – you will be amazed at what it will provide!

Recognise the relationship

The relationship between a family member and their relative has developed throughout all of the latter's life. Recognising the importance and the longevity of this relationship is vital. There will inevitably be a level of interdependence between them. As with most relationships, there may be both positive and negative aspects.

Most families have ups and downs, but these are usually resolved over time with little impact on the relationship. The reality is that the family relationships will continue long after you have moved on.

Recognise the love and their positive intentions

The actions of a parent and other family members are generally borne of love. This is something that can never be replaced by paid staff. Most families want the best for their relatives. It is important to remember that family members generally act with the best of intentions, even if you do not agree with their decisions.

Recognising and acknowledging a family's positive intentions will help you to maintain a wider perspective and will enhance your relationship with family members.

Recognise religious and cultural practices

Each family has their own particular ways of doing things (eg how they spend their time, prepare meals, celebrate together etc.) These are influenced by their culture and for many by their religious practices. It is possible that the cultural and religious experiences of the people you support will be different from your own; you therefore need to recognise these differences and find ways to understand things from the person and their family's perspective.

In working closely with family carers, you will be in a good position to provide the information that really makes a difference, once you have found out from them the most effective way for them to receive and use it. This might include information in their first language, support and information through carers groups, DVDs or culturally informed professionals and peer support. You can find out some more about providing culturally appropriate information in the Mencap (2011) report, *Is Information Enough? Exploring the Information Priorities of Families with a Learning Disability from Pakistani Communities*.

The following activity shows how important it is to find out as much as possible about the people that you are supporting, including their religious beliefs and cultural practices. Without this information, you will only have a partial view of their model of the world.

> **Activity**
>
> Ali, a 19 year old man with a learning disability, moved into supported living six months ago. He has a wonderfully supportive family who are Muslim. The family explained to support staff what was important to them as Muslims and how Ali could be supported, including around what he eats and going to the mosque. This was written down as part of Ali's support plan. However, since moving, Ali has shown a liking for bacon sandwiches, because Jon who he lives with has them every weekend.
>
> *How should staff respond and should this be discussed with Ali's family?*

Some things you need to consider

One issue to be addressed is whether Ali has the capacity to decide whether to eat bacon. If Ali has the capacity to make this decision and has indicated that he wants to eat bacon then this could be judged to be his decision to make, as it would be for any other adult in our society. However, it is not just whether Ali has the capacity to decide 'I like bacon', but also whether he can understand the implications and impact of that choice. For example, it could mean that his family relationships suffer, that he is no longer able to attend the mosque (which might be his main social experience where he meets his friends) or that as a Muslim there would be religious consequences for eating bacon. His family may decide that they want to remove him from his new home because of this issue.

Front line members of staff should not deal with this issue on their own. They should alert their manager who can then review the issues and assess Ali's capacity to make this decision, possibly involving other professionals. This should occur before Ali has the opportunity to actually eat bacon. Ali's support plan will state how he should be supported as a Muslim and should outline the foods that are not normally eaten, together with alternatives for Ali. This could include Halal salted meats that would ensure that Ali did not feel left out at meal times.

If support workers simply allow Ali to eat bacon because they think, 'well it's only a bacon butty, what harm can it do', without any wider discussion and consultation then this could be viewed as an issue for safeguarding as Ali's needs have been neglected.

If Ali is assessed as lacking capacity to decide about eating bacon, in accordance with the mental capacity legislation for the country in which he lives, then a decision has to be made in his 'best interest'. All the relevant people would need to be involved including staff from the flat he shares with Jon, and family members. If appropriate, the local Imam could be asked for advice. One possibility is that the Imam will take the view that, as the person does not understand the consequences of eating bacon, it may not be viewed definitively in a bad way and 'only Allah will judge'. This would mean that Ali would not be ostracised by the Mosque leader for eating bacon and his family may accept this approach. In calling a meeting to discuss the way forward the family may also recognise that the staff are being sensitive to their son's cultural and religious needs.

If Ali is assessed as lacking capacity to decide about eating bacon under the relevant capacity legislation then any meeting will be specifically about this decision. If there are any other issues about Ali and capacity, then a 'best interests' decision and capacity assessment would be required for each instance.

UK mental capacity legislation

It is important to understand the mental capacity laws for the country you work in and their implications for the people you support and their families. Always seek advice from your manager if you have concerns about a person's capacity to make decisions.

In England and Wales

Mental Capacity Act 2005

In Northern Ireland

At the time of writing, mental capacity issues are dealt with under common law although there are plans to introduce capacity legislation

In Scotland

Adults with Incapacity Act (Scotland) 2000

> **Activity**
>
> *Use the internet or a local library to familiarise yourself with the Mental Capacity Act or the relevant laws of the country you work in. Find out about how the law might relate to the needs of the people you support. Or go on a training day about supporting choice and decision making and capacity issues. At a supervision or team meeting share what you find out.*

3. Reassurance

Family members will want to be sure that their relative is receiving the best possible care and support from paid staff. They will want to know that support workers understand their circumstances and have the confidence and expertise to address what needs to happen in any given situation.

Being able to reassure family members is an important factor in creating successful relationships and is linked to providing really good support to the person. However, if the reassurance is found to be unjustified or misplaced, then families are likely to feel let down, leading to a loss of trust and confidence.

Ways to provide reassurance

Follow the support plan The person should already have a support plan that has been developed by the individual together with their family and friends. In supporting the individual to achieve what is in the plan and to have a fulfilling life will provide reassurance for family members.

> The plan we follow is based around our family because family is important to us. For me, it's important that people go back to the plan. Yes, I am the expert but I also want other input as well so that I know that everyone is working towards the best for my brothers, as I am. Once we have agreed on a plan, if things change then we can look at the plan and it is powerful then and you find different things that can alter.
>
> *Kausar Iqbal, sister and family carer to her two brothers with a learning disability*

Be open and transparent Being open, honest and transparent provides a good platform for good relations between you and the family member. This will make them feel able to contribute, confident that they have all of the available information about their family member.

Give feedback Give family members appropriate, timely information and feedback on what has been happening with the person you support. Support the individual to share what they wish with their family.

4. Rapport

Rapport is a quality of harmony and mutual acceptance that exists between some people. We naturally experience rapport with close friends or people who share the same views, beliefs or interests.

> **Thinking point**
>
> *Have you ever met anyone you instantly hit it off with? That was natural rapport.*

Two people in rapport are inclined to be more understanding with each other and more patient. When there is rapport, communication flows easily and it is easier to reach an understanding and to achieve cooperation.

Whilst rapport can happen naturally, working on its development can greatly enhance your communication and relationship with family members. Listening to family members and finding areas of common interest will all help to improve the rapport and therefore the relationship.

> If they are unsure about anything they just phone me up – I prefer it if they do that.
>
> *Kausar Iqbal, sister and family carer to her two brothers with a learning disability*

> **Three steps to develop rapport:**
>
> 1. Make a commitment to develop rapport with family members – it is important that you are genuine and sincere about this. Simply casually going through the motions will come across as false and will not build trust.
>
> 2. Identify a common and shared purpose with the family – this is likely to be supporting the person to have a fulfilling life.
>
> 3. Take a genuine interest in the family. Getting to know the family will help your understanding and will enable you to recognise and respect their views and opinions.

With respect, recognition and reassurance you can create the foundation for the development of ongoing rapport and positive interactions.

For people with autism, there is a need for consistency in terms of activities, routines and how people respond to them. Rapport and understanding between family members and paid staff is very important to maintain this consistency.

> Ceri can be obsessive because of her autism. The staff have used me to teach them how to work through the obsessions – sometimes they just give me a call or I attend staff meetings and this helps to avoid upsets. Liz the manager has written up in a book – if this happens with Ceri, this is what you do. We all have to follow the same plan so that Ceri has consistency – we all have to sing from the same song sheet. That way Ceri is happier.
>
> Support can go both ways – one day Ceri's support worker phoned me and said 'I'm going into anaphylactic shock.' I ran up there to support Ceri whilst her husband picked her up and took her to hospital. So its swings and roundabouts – they know I'm there for them and I know they are there for Ceri and they support her very well.
>
> *Christine, Ceri's mum*

Demonstrating dependability in carrying out any actions agreed with families

Thinking point

Your 10 year old washing machine broke down last week. You have taken the day off work to take delivery of the new washing machine that you ordered and paid for at the weekend. There is a pile of laundry waiting to be done. At 1 o'clock there is a phone call to say that they cannot deliver today after all and that the next time that they will be in your area is next week. What do you say? How do you feel?

It is always disappointing when something that you have been promised does not happen. If it is something as significant as your relative not having gone out for the day because no one was available to support them or that there has been a missed hospital appointment because it had not been entered in the diary, it is easy to feel let down.

As a staff member, you will need to be able to demonstrate that you can be relied on to follow a person's support plan consistently over time and to do what you say you will do on a day to day basis, unless there are any unforeseen reasons why this is not possible.

An important rule of thumb is to 'under promise and over deliver'. In other words do not promise to do anything that you know you cannot fulfil.

You need to demonstrate that you can be relied on to follow a person's support plan.

> A lot of family carers feel let down by paid staff when they're not kept up to date with what's happening. If paid staff would recognise our frustration then we would feel less antagonistic towards them, things would be less fraught. If they tried to understand our position, think about where we're coming from, respect us as individuals and communicate with us effectively it might help us understand their shortcomings.
>
> *Pauline Rogers, Alison's mum*

Written or spoken communication is again the key to making sure that colleagues know about any actions that have been agreed with family members. Regular and ongoing communication with family members is equally important, including letting them know why something agreed does not happen for any reason.

Describe the principles for addressing dilemmas or conflicts that may arise in relationships with families

Disagreements and conflicts can happen for many different reasons. This can be because people see things very differently because of their perspective and their role in relation to the person being supported. Sometimes, conflict can be constructive – it can help to clarify or resolve important issues or people's roles and responsibilities. Conflict can help to release pent-up stress, anxiety or emotion.

However, conflict can also be damaging to relationships and can divert attention away from important issues. It can damage the morale and confidence of both paid staff and family members. It can also have a negative impact on the individual being supported, who may find themselves caught in the crossfire. Conflict is a major source of stress and illness. Dealing positively with disagreements and conflict is a skill that can take time to develop and hone.

> **Activity**
>
> Think about a situation that you have been involved in or witnessed where there was significant conflict between two people.
> - What was the conflict about?
> - How were the people communicating?
> - What emotions did you witness?
> - How was the conflict ended or resolved?
> - Who played a major part in resolving the conflict and how did they behave?
> - What was the relationship between the two people like after the conflict was resolved?

> Whenever you're in conflict with someone, there is one factor that can make the difference between damaging your relationship and deepening it. That factor is attitude.
>
> *William James*

Important principles and skills for resolving conflict include:

- conflict and anger management;
- listening;
- negotiation;
- mediation – looking for areas of agreement and identifying information such as legal constraints;
- facilitation.

Different ways of handling conflict

All of us have to deal with conflict in a whole range of situations and with different people at different times. As a paid worker, you need to be aware of your own approach to handling conflict and also be aware of alternative strategies that you could use.

In any situation where you and a family member disagree it is crucial that you listen to and show your respect for their views, even if they are different to your own.

There are five main approaches to handling conflict which are:

1. Competing

is being assertive and uncooperative. This is where someone pursues their own concerns at the expense of someone else; using whatever power they have to achieve their own ends. Competing can mean standing up for your rights, defending a position that you believe is correct, or simply trying to win at all costs.

2. Accommodating

means the person is unassertive and cooperative and appears to virtually give in. An accommodating person tries to preserve the relationship between the parties at all costs, stressing areas of agreement and often failing to confront any difficult issues.

3. Avoiding

means being unassertive but uncooperative in not addressing the issues or the conflict. Avoiding may lead to sidestepping the issue, postponing discussions until a later date or simply withdrawing.

4. Compromising

is midway between assertiveness and cooperativeness and between competing and accommodating. The goal is to find solutions which satisfy both parties. The issues are addressed more directly than in avoiding but not as thoroughly as in joint problem solving. This approach views conflict as best resolved by cooperation and compromise.

5. Joint problem solving

is both assertive and cooperative – the opposite of avoiding. It involves working together to identify each other's concerns, learning from each other's insights and finding a solution that meets the concerns of both parties.

> **Activity**
>
> *Which is your usual style of resolving conflict? Is it appropriate to your work situation? If not, which other styles might you use to resolve a disagreement between a family carer and yourself? Discuss your ideas with your line manager at your next supervision.*

Key points from this chapter

- Interact with families in ways that respect their culture, experience and expertise.
- The 4R's will help you to establish and maintain positive relationships – Respect, Recognition, Reassurance, Rapport.
- With respect, recognition and reassurance you can create the foundation for rapport to take place.
- It is important to respect and follow the person's support plan and communicate progress and timely information to family members.
- It is important to understand your approaches to handling conflict to ensure that if conflict does arise it is dealt with in a positive way.
- It is important to maintain regular, open, timely, ongoing communication with family members.

References and where to go for more information

References

Hatton, S and Boughton, T (2011) *An Introduction to Supporting People with Autistic Spectrum Conditions.* Exeter: Learning Matters/BILD

Hatton, S and Simpson, J (2012) *Next Steps in Supporting People with Autistic Spectrum Conditions.* London: Sage/Learning Matters/BILD

James, William from: www.simplyaninspiredlife.com

Mencap (2011) *Is Information Enough? Exploring the Information Priorities of Families with a Learning Disability from Pakistani Communities.* London: Mencap

Legislation, policies and reports

All UK legislation can be downloaded from www.legislation.gov.uk

Policies and reports for Northern Ireland, Scotland and Wales can be found at www.northernireland.gov.uk, www.scotland.gov.uk and www.wales.gov.uk respectively. Policies and reports for England can be found on the website of the relevant government department.

Mental Capacity Act (2005) – applies to England and Wales

Adults with Incapacity (Scotland) Act (2000)

Northern Ireland currently does not have mental capacity legislation. Mental capacity issues are dealt with under common law. Mental capacity legislation is likely to be introduced in 2014.

Websites

Hft Family Carer Support Services www.hft.org.uk/familycarersupport

National Family Carer Network www.familycarers.org.uk

Chapter 4

Planned shared approaches to the care and support of individuals with families

> One support worker working to positively involve families says:
>
> In my experience it's about getting a feel for families by working with them and their experiences and by keeping them involved as much as is possible. One of my most positive experiences was when I worked alongside the sister of a gentleman who had previously not had that much involvement with her brother. She took part in the person centred plan and was amazed at the possibilities for him and really enjoyed being with her brother.
>
> *Richard Wood, support worker and family member*

Person centred planning finds out what is important to the person.

Introduction

Chapter 3 was about attitudes and approaches to partnerships. This chapter will help you to think about how the practicalities of successful partnership work. It stresses the importance of communicating well with family carers so that there is clarity about everyone's roles and responsibilities to avoid misunderstandings.

You will recall in Chapter 1, the importance of agreeing from the start:

- how the partnership will work in practice;
- how everyone will know that partnership working is happening and is working well;
- how it will be reviewed;
- how successes will be recorded;
- how any difficulties will be resolved.

Agreeing the outcomes of working together with the person and their family is important. This will enable everyone to measure how well the support provided has worked and the success or otherwise of the partnership between paid staff and family members. It is also important that everyone involved in the person's support is clear about their own role and the role of others; this needs to be discussed and agreed.

Each person's support plan should set out the planned outcomes and identify how they will be achieved and how any risks will be managed. Working in partnership with family members will include agreements about how the plan will be mutually delivered, monitored and updated.

Learning Outcomes

This chapter will help you to:

- agree with the individual, family members and others the proposed outcomes of partnership working with a family;
- clarify your own role, the role of family members, and the roles of others in supporting the individual;

- support family members to understand person centred approaches and agreed ways of working;
- plan ways to manage any risks associated with sharing care or support;
- agree the processes for monitoring the shared support plan with the individual and family members.

This chapter covers:

Level 3 HSC 3038 – Work in partnership with families to support individuals: Learning Outcome 3

Agree the proposed outcomes of partnership working with a family

When supporting a person with a learning disability or a person with autism, the main goal for everyone involved will be achieving a meaningful and fulfilling life for the person. Outcomes towards this should be set in the support plan.

When you start working with someone, you will expect to be given a job description that will include some details of the hours that you will work which may vary, the activities that you will undertake and the details of your role as part of the person's wider support network. Other people who may already have a role in supporting the person will probably include fellow support workers, a team leader or manager, friends and family members alongside medical and other professionals and staff from other agencies.

Where are the outcomes set out for the person you support?

Everyone should be working to a person centred plan drawn up by the person you support with help from those closest to them, usually the person's family. This plan should include the individual's wishes and desires and an outline of their regular routines and activities. It should identify the way in which they want their support to be provided, including meeting any healthcare needs, and say what types of decisions they can make alone as well as who might help with supported decision-making. It should also include information about the important people in the person's life (including family members) with contact details and how they are involved in their life. Most people also have a support plan that is a document used every day by those supporting them. A support plan provides more detailed information about the person's day to day support needs and should be used by workers, and others, to inform what they do.

Where do you fit within the person's person centred plan and support plan?

You will have been employed to support a person for a range of different reasons. Probably you have been employed by an organisation or the person and their circle of support, and were selected after an interview which took into account your knowledge, skills and abilities, trustworthiness and values. You may have been identified as the right person to support someone as you matched the kind of supporter that their plan had identified as being suitable.

Using such a matching process can help the person, their family and the organisation supporting them to identify the right person to meet their needs and wishes and to give them a fulfilling life. Family members are likely to be well placed to work with the person requiring support to draw up a profile of the type of person to be recruited.

You can find out more about person centred approaches and values in the book by Liz Tilly (2011) *Person Centred Approaches when Supporting People with a Learning Disability*, in this series.

Thinking point

If you were unfit and uninterested in hill walking would it be appropriate for you to support someone who really enjoyed that activity?

> **Activity**
>
> *Using the framework, headings and examples below, identify your interests, personality, capabilities and skills and create an imaginary person who would benefit from your support.*
>
> | Support wanted and needed | Capabilities and skills needed | Personality type needed | Shared interests |
> |---|---|---|---|
> | To go hill walking | Fit and a good sense of direction | Motivated and chatty | Walking and nature |
> | To go to college | A driver | Someone who is flexible | Photography |
> | To work on my plan | Be able to use a computer | Interested in other people | My future |

Sharing information – agreements and confidentiality

You may be employed by a family member on behalf of someone, by an organisation or by the person themselves. In all of these situations it is important to make an agreement in principle about sharing information with the person and their family members. Such an agreement is important in developing and maintaining trust with both the person and their family members.

An agreement of roles, responsibilities and the support outcomes can be formally set out in the support plan or may be in an informal arrangement between the individual, you and

A matching process can help the person identify the right support to meet their needs to give them a fulfilling life.

Planning shared approaches to the care and support of individuals with families   **67** the family member. However it is planned or recorded, it is very important that the way in which you work and share information with other partners and especially family members should be clear. Being clear about what and how information is shared is important in keeping within the law, building trust with the person you support and with their family in avoiding differing expectations. By keeping to the agreement you will demonstrate that you are reliable and dependable and that you are committed to person centred support.

Not all family members share everything about their life with the rest of their family. Many of us take part in activities that we would not like our parents or siblings to know about or we may tell one family member something in confidence that we do not want shared with other family members. However, there are some families who are very open and share everything with each other. As we have already discussed, every family is different and will have different expectations about what should be shared and what should not.

Confidentiality is important to all of us, and will be for the person that you are supporting. You should know about and follow the confidentiality policies and procedures of the organisation that you work for. You should never use confidentiality as an excuse to exclude families from being involved (Northumberland, Tyne and Wear NHS Foundation Trust, 2010). If you are unsure about what you are able to share with others about the person you support you should seek advice from your line manager.

The person you support may want privacy in some areas of their life and may ask that their family is not always informed or told about certain issues. This can place paid staff in the difficult situation of maintaining the person's confidence whilst working in partnership with their family. If all parties have agreed what sort of information is to be shared and what kept confidential there is less likelihood of such tension.

So when should you keep things confidential on behalf of the person that you are supporting? If you work for an organisation it is important that you are aware of their policies and procedures on confidentiality and co-operating with other providers. The Care Quality Commission, in England, and the other inspection organisations in the other UK countries, makes confidentiality part of their core standards that health and social care organisations must comply with. Your organisation's written policies and procedures will have to comply with the inspection regulations, both the people you support and family members should know about these policies and have them available in a format they understand.

> ### Thinking point
>
> *Ian lives in a flat close to his mother, Marie. Marie was really happy with her son's new support staff – he had bonded well with them and they seemed more like friends to him than employees. Ian has had problems with his feet since childhood and needs to wear 'good shoes that provide support' so that he doesn't get pains in his feet that then further affects his mobility. He has needed some new shoes for a while and he really liked the fashionable trainers of Alec his favourite support worker. Alec and Ian went out to buy his new shoes and ended up getting a pair of trainers the same as Alec's. Unfortunately these were too narrow for Ian's feet, caused him pain and ended up being given to the charity shop. Alec had gone with Ian to spend his money without prior discussion with his mother. From this fairly expensive experience everyone learnt that Marie's insistence on 'sensible shoes' was important and so future choices would probably be supported better.*
>
> *If you were supporting Ian what would you have done?*

Reaching agreement on what is to be shared can identify the principles of confidentiality between the person you support, the family member and you. Agreeing what should be shared is easier than what should be kept confidential because it can be difficult to agree in advance about specific activities that are to be kept confidential as it might mean breaking confidentiality. If you feel that you are in a dilemma in relation to confidentially speak to your line manager or a senior colleague to get advice.

What will be agreed will differ between families and it is important to recognise that your role in partnership working with families does not mean controlling the relationship between the person and their family; in fact, your role is to support the person within their relationships with family members.

Shared approaches to decision making

If the person you support wishes, other people can work with them when they are making decisions about their present and future choices. They can get support from friends, paid staff and family members; good person centred planning can shape the way this is done.

When supporting someone with choices and decision making, family members may provide 'ordinary' solutions that you may not be in a position to offer. In these situations the partnership between you and the family members can create a robust support mechanism to the person increasing the choices available.

In looking at decision making, it can be helpful to separate decisions into everyday or major decisions.

Everyday decisions are those that are made regularly and support our lifestyle. They include what we do on a daily basis such as choosing our clothes, what to have for lunch, which television programme to watch or choosing whether to have tea or coffee.

Major decisions are made less frequently but have a greater impact on our life. They often require more thought and planning and you may need advice or to share the decision making with someone else. These could include making decisions about a change in accommodation or who to live with, applying for a new job, going away on a holiday, getting married, opening a bank account or making an expensive purchase.

Everyday decisions are those made regularly and support our lifestyle.

Understanding when a decision is major is not always obvious. What would be an everyday choice for some people might be a major decision for someone else. For some people with autism walking into a busy restaurant with lots of noise may be confusing and distressing, but because they really want to go to a celebration lunch, choosing this type of eating out could present a major decision for them.

A good support plan, learning from colleagues and partnership working with family members, should help provide you with the information you need to support the person with decision making, so that where possible they will have the choices and opportunities to have a fulfilling life.

Activity

Identify two recent examples of everyday and major decisions in your own life.

What impact did those decisions have on you? Did you involve anyone else in making any of those decisions?

Thinking point

Sarah had been supported in her new home by staff for two months. Things had been going really well with her personal assistants who had a very positive relationship with her. Sarah was enjoying her life and, as a young woman in her mid 20s, was developing her self esteem and confidence. She told her personal assistants she would like to have a new hairstyle like one that she had seen in a magazine. They supported her to go to the hairdressers and have the new style which was shorter than usual. Sarah was delighted and thought it would be a nice surprise for her mum to see the next day.

When her mum saw Sarah's new hairstyle she was angry and told the PAs that they should have asked her as she had always taken Sarah to the hairdressers.

- *What could have been done to avoid this situation?*
- *Was Sarah making an everyday or a major decision?*

One positive way to reaching a shared approach to making and supporting decisions is to work together with the person you support, and the people they want to be involved, to write a simple chart such as the one below.

Decisions in my life	Who must be involved and who can support me?	Who makes the final decision?
Setting my household budget for food shopping	Although I know the food I like and my mum and Andy my support worker will support me to make a list, I don't always know much about the money side of shopping.	Mum
Getting new staff to support me	I have said in my support plan about the type of person I am looking for and they must like to do some of the same things I like.	Mum and me
Where I go on holiday	Andy will support me to save through the year. He will help me to choose somewhere within my budget by showing me the brochures and I will choose.	Me

Keeping the person safe and well

It is unlikely you will feel happy if you do not feel safe. An important part of someone's person centred plan and support plan will be how they will remain safe and well. This will often be at the forefront of the minds of family members and addressing these issues together in partnership will help families to be less anxious and worried about their relative.

Planning ahead in partnership with families should include looking at all eventualities including what to do in an emergency. If staff cover is delayed or absent for any reason, there needs to be an agreed response. Arrangements might be made with a family member about who to contact so that their relative, the person you support is never left in a vulnerable position. If you work for an organisation, then it is more likely that your line manager will need to be contacted so they can respond to any situation and inform the family as necessary. This planning should also include who to contact in case of a medical emergency, car accident, etc.

Keeping the person safe and well might also include supporting the person to know when they are unwell. The individual may require support to understand when they are unwell or to recognise any early signs of illness. You may be able to work together with family members to ensure vigilance and awareness. Family members will often have important knowledge of the indicators that have shown ill health in the past, particularly if it is a recurring illness or health condition.

An important part of a person's support plan is how they will stay safe and well.

> Leanne will say 'I've got a headache', but you have got to ask her where she has a headache – and it could be in her stomach because she uses the word headache for pain. I am with Leanne all the time and I have picked up all this information over the years. Parents can and need to pass on information like this.
>
> *Lynne, Leanne's mum*

Knowing the complexities of the person's needs is part of keeping a person safe and well. For example, the person may have developed particular ways of behaving and interacting with the world and the people around them. This may include various rituals or routines or individual ways of communication and having a good understanding of these will often alleviate anxieties for the person. Family members' detailed knowledge of their relative can be invaluable in helping you and colleagues to understand their relative and to support them to keep safe and well.

> **Activity**
>
> *Your organisation has just started supporting Chris, who until recently lived at home with his parents. Chris loves washing up and prides himself on doing it well. He has a ritual around washing up that other people may not even notice unless they accidentally spoil his routine. He has a particular order in which he chooses to wash the dishes, pots and pans and this must be followed. If anyone disrupts his ritual by putting dirty pots in the washing up bowl, then Chris may become upset, angry or even verbally abusive. Unless you know about his washing up routine, Chris's anger and distress may appear to come from nowhere and to be out of proportion to what has happened. How might you find out about the complexity of Chris's needs? Discuss your ideas with a senior colleague or your line manager.*

Clarifying your own role, the role of family members, and the roles of others in supporting the individual

Your first responsibility as a paid worker is to follow your job description which will focus on delivering the person's support plan; it should explain what is expected of you in the support you provide.

Being clear about who does what in supporting the person is likely to result in a more successful partnership with families than leaving things to chance. For example, it may be that a family member has always gone with their relative to hospital or GP appointments in the past. Rather than assuming that you will now take over this role, it is important to talk about it together and decide with the person who they would prefer to do this with in future. The outcome should be included in the person's health action plan. It is very important that whoever supports the person with health appointments has an agreed way of sharing information about what happened and what are the outcomes. This will then ensure that any follow up or treatment is carried out, always with the person's knowledge and consent.

The person's support plan should include the names of the people who will support them to do specific things. This should be reviewed and updated on a regular basis. Changes in who supports the person may happen quite naturally as part of their growing independence and their wanting to make more choices. As family members develop trust in the support provided for their relative, they may want to take less responsibility themselves.

As support staff, you will need to work together with the family. Although they may appear over protective or disinterested to you at times, you must remember that their previous experiences may not always have been positive. Get alongside them and listen to them carefully. In this way, you will learn valuable information that will help you support the person.

> Sometimes I come over as over protective because I can't do things as I always did but because I see her progressing I can see that I have to leave some things alone. It's hard to take a step back after all those years!
>
> *Christine, Ceri's mum*

It is always better to discuss any possible areas for misunderstanding or disagreement with families before they become big issues. This is respectful to family members and means that major problems between families and staff are more likely to be avoided.

> We can talk about positive and negative aspects of the support and discuss them and how we can work through the negative. We have odd disagreements and sometimes I am in the wrong and sometimes staff has been in the wrong.
>
> *Christine, Ceri's mum*

Supporting family members who do not already know about person centred approaches

Being person centred with values that promote individuality in terms of choice, rights, independence and inclusion should be at the centre of your role. A person centred approach means that everything you do is based upon what is important to the individual person that requires support. One of the best ways of achieving this is by carrying out person centred planning with the person and those they choose to be involved in the process. Person centred planning finds out what the person wants and how they want it delivered and by whom.

> Person centred planning is a process for continual listening and learning, focussing on what is important to someone now and in the future, and acting upon this in alliance with their family and friends.
>
> *Helen Sanderson Associates from www.helensandersonassociates.co.uk*

A key principle of person centred planning is that families and friends are full and equal partners in planning, if that's what the person wants, and the person is viewed as being part of a family and their wider community. A person centred approach assumes that a family member's involvement will make a rich contribution to the individual.

> Staff can use jargonistic language but it's important that we all speak in a way that everyone understands – that way Angie gets the best care.
>
> *Frank and Judi Lunt, Angie's dad and mum*

Even if they have never heard the term 'person centred approaches', or be familiar with the different tools or planning formats, it is important to note that family carers are likely to have been working in a person centred way all of the person's life. However, they may well have felt that they were doing this on their own and in isolation. One of the best features of partnership working with a family is that individuals are more likely to receive the best quality of support possible when all parties can put their knowledge and ideas together.

Involving family members in the planning process at a level that suits them helps to avoid any unexpected misunderstandings. Person centred planning is built on inclusion and looks at what support a person needs to be included and involved in their local community. The following features are central to such planning:

- the person is at the centre;
- family members and friends are full partners;
- the planning focuses upon the person's capacities, what is important to them and identifies the support they need to make a contribution to their local community;
- a shared commitment to action from those involved in the planning;
- a continual process of listening, learning and action.

There are a number of different planning approaches and tools that are based upon person centred principles. These include:

Essential Lifestyle Planning (ELP): a process for learning how someone wants to live and developing a plan that makes this happen.

It was originally developed to support people, often with no relatives actively involved in their lives, who were moving out of institutions into their communities. An ELP is developed by spending time with and listening to the person and others who know and care about them. Learning about what is important to this person and what support they need is captured and used.

> Developing plans that really reflect how people want to live requires the perspectives of those who know and love the person; listening to what they like and admire about the person: and their stories of good days and bad. Learning how people want to live is just the beginning; a plan provides the framework of our on-going learning.
>
> *Helen Sanderson Associates from www.helensandersonassociates.co.uk*

Personal Futures Planning: a planning process that focuses on getting to know the person and what their life is like now, then developing ideas about what they would like in the future. The plan identifies what action is necessary to move towards this and explores the opportunities in the community and what needs to change in services. This takes place with a group of people who are committed to the person and the process and normally includes the family and friends.

PATH (Planning Alternative Tomorrows with Hope): an approach which focuses on a future that is desirable, often based on a dream or goal for the future, and encourages direct action and enrolment of participants to make actions happen. This is a helpful approach when the issues are complex and external supports and resources are likely to be required.

MAP: is a tool and process that helps a person and their family, friends and others close to them, to identify their history, dreams, nightmares, gifts, strengths, talents and needs and then turn them into an action plan. This focuses on the people and resources needed to move towards the dreams and away from nightmares.

Support planning for a personal budget: in order to obtain a personal budget people normally need a person centred support plan that shows how they will direct their own support. The local authority will need details of how the person will use the money to get adequate and safe support. Some individuals may wish to use this information to guide their support and use it as a basis for ongoing planning.

The involvement of families in the planning processes and ongoing support is now recognised as good practice, particularly because of what they bring in skills, knowledge, experience and ongoing love and commitment for their relative. However, many families will have lived through times when some services supporting people with a learning disability and people with autism adopted a 'professionals know best' approach and made little effort to work with families as partners or to make them feel welcome in the person's life. This has led to some families feeling that they have been removed from any involvement in their relative's life or support. They talk of having to battle to remain involved or to receive any information about their relative from staff or service providers.

Managing risks associated with sharing care or support

> Risk means the likelihood of an event or circumstances occurring which can cause harm to the person involved or to other people...
>
> *Liz Tilly, from Person Centred Approaches when Supporting People with a Learning Disability (2011)*

People with learning disabilities and people with autism have often been prevented from having fulfilling lives due to concerns about the risks involved. Both family carers and service providers have adopted over cautious approaches that identify various real and imagined consequences. Service providers have developed increasingly complicated ways to assess risks where avoiding blame can seem more important than taking time to mitigate the risks and enable positive experiences.

Concerns about risk taking are often deeply held and this can lead to individual staff, service providers and families being passionate about their position and views which can make agreement of what to do difficult to achieve.

In *Person Centred Approaches when Supporting People with a Learning Disability* (2011), Liz Tilly identifies that when people do not have the opportunity to take risks, we:

- deny them their rights as equal and valued adults;
- deny them the right to control their own life and make their own decisions;
- deprive them of valuable and enjoyable experiences and deny new opportunities;
- reduce their ability to deal with unforeseen risks that they will inevitably encounter in life;
- prevent them learning new things or meeting new people;
- make people dependent and passive;
- ignore individual needs and differences;

- restrict lives and possibly create frustration which can lead to challenging behaviour;
- prevent them from learning from their experiences.

> **Activity**
>
> *Think of someone that you support and what happens when they wish to do something that might involve some risk. What is your role and the role of their family in any decisions that are made? Is there a potential conflict between your duty of care and the individual's right to live the life that they want? Discuss your ideas with a senior colleague or your line manager.*

Government policy has recognised that a purposeful life inevitably includes risk taking.

> It should be possible for a person to have a support plan which enables them to manage identified risks and to live their lives in ways which best suit them.
>
> *Independence, Choice and Risk; A Guide to Best Practice in Supported Decision Making (Department of Health, 2007)*

If people are to be supported to take control over their lives and to make their choices and decisions, then they will need to benefit from positive and informed risk taking. This starts from a commitment to overcoming any identified risks and finding solutions rather than simply ruling things out.

The involvement of families and the views and perspectives of family carers is very important.

> ...The purpose of any risk assessment is just as much about the happiness of the person, their family and the community as it is about their safety.
>
> *Neill, Allen, Woodhead, Reid, Irwin and Sanderson (2008)*

Keeping the person at the centre of any risk assessment and planning and ensuring that their family and friends are seen as experts and partners will make sure that their potential is achieved without compromising their safety.

Families will be able to share what has happened previously and what lessons have been learnt. Their perspective will help generate ideas and solutions to enable the person to achieve what is important to them whilst considering what keeps them and their community safe.

Your job will be to support the person to undertake activities in such a way that any risks are positively managed as far as possible. Good communication between everyone involved in supporting the person will be essential in drawing up a planned approach to risk, ensuring that everyone understands any risks involved and that there is consistency in how the risk is managed.

If you are employed by the person and their family using a personal budget they will probably have a support plan that explains what the person will be supported to do and their aspirations for the future. The plan should include details of how the person will be kept safe, highlighting any risks and stating how they will be managed. If there is no clear plan you may need to negotiate with your employer how any risks will be managed, always bearing in mind the importance of supported decision making to include the person themselves in this. With good communication, partnership working with family members will enhance the support given to the individual, keep them safe and well, and reduce risks.

Thinking point

You are supporting someone who wants to learn how to travel on the bus into town by herself so that she can go shopping independently at the weekend. How would you ensure that the risks involved were identified and addressed and that her family were fully involved in the process?

The person's support plan will be a living document and how it is implemented, monitored and evaluated will vary for each individual. Having an agreement about how the family will be involved in monitoring the plan is important for:

- partnership working with families;
- you to know that you are doing a good job;
- ensuring that the person is getting the agreed support;
- making changes as required.

The shared support plan will identify who is doing what and when, and set agreed times when all involved will meet to look at the plan and work out what is working and what changes might be needed.

> **Activity**
>
> *Find your employer's risk assessment policy and procedures. Check that they explain how people with a learning disability and people with autism and their families and friends know about the policy and how they will be involved in the decision making process. Are there ways in which the policy and procedures could be changed to improve the inclusion of family and friends? Share your thoughts with your line manager.*

Supervision

Supervision is an important right and benefit for all those working in social care. It is the main way in which your organisation monitors and reviews your work but also ensures you are properly supported and continue to develop your skills.

Skills for Care and Children's Workforce Development Council (2007)

If you are employed by the person and their family, you will receive supervision, either from a family or circle of support member, or a more senior worker employed by them to take on this responsibility. The supervisor should be approachable and available, and be able to provide feedback on your performance, help you to clarify your priorities and goals and provide a forum for discussion on how to deliver quality support.

Supervision time is a good opportunity to monitor the support plan – a senior worker is likely to have more experience with the person and their family. There may also be joint meetings of all personal assistants or paid staff working with the person to look at how the support plan is working.

The person and the family may use an external organisation to support and supervise the personal assistants or other paid staff. Such external organisations can provide a person centred planning service for families and may support you to work in partnership with the family on how the plan will be monitored.

You may be employed by an organisation that has a supervision system in place. Your supervisor will provide support and ideas on how to work positively with the family.

Key working

If you work as part of a team that supports lots of people in one place, you may be given the role of a key worker. This means acting as the lead member of staff for an individual to ensure that their needs and wishes are met. This will give you an ideal opportunity to agree a process with the person you are key worker to and their family on how to monitor the support plan's delivery.

As a key worker, you will usually be the first point of contact for the family. This will mean that you will actively liaise with the person's family and friends in ways that promote open communication and feedback.

Ongoing feedback

For some people, regularly updating and developing their support plan is an enjoyable and valued part of their routine. This is a great way for the person to stay in control. In addition, you will be in a good position to involve family members in the updating of the plan and ensuring their contributions. Working in partnership in this way will ensure that all parties are included and share their knowledge and expertise in a positive way.

Key points from this chapter

- The main outcome to which everyone involved should be working is a meaningful, fulfilling life for the person being supported.

- Everyone should understand their specific role in supporting the person, right from the start. This planned approach can result in a more successful partnership than leaving things to chance.

- Making an agreement in principle about sharing information with the person and their family members is important in maintaining trust with everyone.

- Setting out how the person will be supported to make decisions and who will give this support will make it easier for everyone to understand their role.

- Positive risk taking should ensure that families and friends are fully involved with the person and able to share their knowledge, experience and views.

- The person's support plan should be a living document – everyone needs to agree with the person how the plan will be kept alive, monitored, evaluated and amended.

- Good communication is critical to effective partnership working.

References and where to go for more information

References

Department of Health (2007) *Independence, Choice and Risk; A Guide to Best Practice in Supported Decision Making.* London: Department of Health

Hatton, S (2011) *An Introduction to Supporting People with Autistic Spectrum Conditions.* Exeter: Learning Matters/BILD

Smull, M and Sanderson, H (2005) *Essential Lifestyle Planning For Everyone.* Toronto: Canada Inclusion Press

Pearpoint, J, O'Brien, J and Forest, M (1991) *Planning Positive Possible Futures, Planning Alternative Tomorrows with Hope (PATH).* Toronto: Canada Inclusion Press

National Family Carer Network and HFT (2012) *Making sure your Relative is Safe. Top Tips for Family Carers about 'Safeguarding' Adults with Learning Disabilities.* Downloadable from: www.hft.org.uk/safeguarding

Neill, M, Allen, J, Woodhead, N, Reid, S, Irwin, L and Sanderson, H (2008) *A Positive Approach to Risk Requires Person Centred Thinking.* Stockport: Helen Sanderson Associates

Northumberland, Tyne and Wear NHS Foundation Trust (2010)
Commonsense Confidentiality. A Guide for Carers, Family and Friends.
Downloadable from: www.ntw.nhs.uk/pic

Skills for Care and Children's Workforce Development Council (2007)
Providing Effective Supervision. A Workforce Development Tool, Including a Unit of Competence and Supporting Guidance. Leeds: Skills for Care/Children's Workforce Development Council

Tilly, L (2011) *Person Centred Approaches when Supporting People with a Learning Disability.* Exeter: Learning Matters/BILD

Websites

Helen Sanderson Associates www.helensandersonassociates.co.uk

Hft Family Carer Support Services www.hft.org.uk

Inclusion Network www.inclusion.com

National Family Carer Network www.familycarers.org.uk

Support Planning www.supportplanning.org

Social Care Institute for Excellence – Social Care TV www.scie.org.uk/socialcaretv

Chapter 5

Working with families to enable them to access support in their role as carers

> It means a lot that my views about my daughter's support are listened to and respected in her reviews. But they don't give my needs as a family carer much thought. It's me who has to remind them that I'm getting older and can't be as involved in her life now. After years of being involved I'm now in my 70s and I'm trying to be less involved in my daughter's life.
>
> My daughter's care manager also came to do my carer's assessment which I felt was a conflict of interest. It was a waste of time… nothing happened… They know we'll never leave our sons and daughters.
>
> It would be so much easier for all of us – the person, paid staff and family members – if they recognised our expertise and listened to us. For lots of family carers it gets personal because they feel they don't have a chance to be heard.
>
> *Pauline Rogers, Alison's mum*

Introduction

This chapter emphasises the importance of family members having access to practical and emotional support and understandable information to support them in their carer's role. This means identifying the particular information that each family and family member requires. You can do this while offering family members an understanding and supportive relationship, this can then lead to greater confidence in the support being provided and an increased willingness to share concerns or worries.

As a paid worker, it is important that you know about how and where to obtain information and support for family members, then you can pass this on appropriately. This chapter will help you to learn about the support that is available for family carers and the different ways to make this available to people when they need it.

> ### Learning Outcomes
>
> This chapter will help you to:
>
> - work with family members to identify the support they need to carry out their role;
> - provide accessible information about available sources of support;
> - challenge information or support that is discriminatory or inaccessible;
> - work with family members to access resources;
> - provide feedback to others about the support accessed by family members and report on any gaps in the provision of support for family members.
>
> ### This chapter covers:
>
> Level 3 HSC 3038 – Work in partnership with families to support individuals: Learning Outcomes 4 and 7

Work with family members to identify the support they need to carry out their role

Carers often end up having to juggle the support they give with their other responsibilities, in a difficult balancing act. For many carers, looking after their own health, combining caring with work, getting access to training or simply having time to take a break or go away for a weekend can be a major challenge. Government research on carers shows that people who provide a substantial amount of care tend to have lower incomes, poorer health and are less likely to be in work than their counterparts.

Department of Health, 2008

In Chapter 1 you learnt about the *Common Core Principles for Working with Carers* developed by Skills for Care and Skills for Health (2011). It is worth revisiting them once more and thinking through which of the principles are most relevant when working with family members to enable them to access support in their role as a carer.

> The key principles that should guide your work are:
>
> **Principle 3:** Support carers to be as physically and mentally as well as possible and prevent ill health.
>
> In practice this means:
>
> - workers will have awareness and understanding that carers can often have poorer physical and mental health than that of the general population and miss out on opportunities to keep well due to their caring role;
>
> - workers will promote and offer opportunities to enable carers to 'stay at their best' by identifying support needs that enable a life outside caring;
>
> - workers will recognise and value that carers have roles outside of caring and enable carers to maintain valued relationships and interests.
>
> **Principle 6:** Respect and recognise that carers will have their own support needs, rights and aspirations, which may be different from that of the cared for person.
>
> In practice this means:
>
> - workers will recognise that carers are also individuals who have needs themselves and workers should always strive to understand these needs and respond in a way that reflects individual needs and/or choices;
>
> - workers should recognise that this may at times involve an assessment of risk and the need to respond appropriately and manage this proportionately;
>
> - workers will recognise that carers have legal rights, including a right to an assessment of need in their own right.
>
> **Principle 8:** Recognise the experience of carers as the caring role ends and after it has ended, offer support to carers accordingly.

> In practice this means:
>
> - carers needs' will change as the person they care for either no longer needs their care, the carer no longer provides the care or the cared for person dies;
> - workers will recognise these changing needs, the support required and the potential on-going nature of this support.

Activity

Read through the three principles again and consider how well you, and any organisation you work for, practically demonstrate that you keep to these principles. Discuss the principles, or you could demonstrate how you maintain them, at your next team meeting, or in your next supervision.

The support that family members need to carry out their role

Each family member will have their own particular individual needs in addition to those that relate to their role as a family carer. These can easily be overlooked because of the priority that family members will invariably give to their caring role.

Caring can be very stressful and demanding for a family member. It can be difficult to achieve a balance between maintaining the health and well being of the relative being cared for and their own needs. However, family carers who look after their own physical and emotional well being are likely to be better able to cope with the ongoing demands of caring.

The support that family carers require will depend on many different factors. This will include the context in which they are supporting a family member, which can include:

- whether their relative still lives in the family home;
- whether the carer still provides most of the day to day support needed by their relative;
- whether the person is living in their own home, in supported living or in residential care but the family carer is still involved;

- whether the family carer is the employer for paid staff supporting the person.

Family members' knowledge of the availability of support, their awareness of opportunities for their relative and their willingness to take risks will vary. Over the years, some families will have gathered considerable knowledge and creative expertise, whilst others may have struggled with the day to day caring and been unable to look far beyond this. It is always important for paid staff to be able to relate to each family member's unique experience and respond with empathy and understanding. This will then avoid the danger of responding with assumptions, generalisations or stereotyping.

Most family members will welcome an opportunity to discuss how they would like to be involved in their son or daughter's life, both now and in the future. It will be important that these discussions take into account the wishes of their relatives. In addition, it must be recognised that families come from diverse backgrounds and each will have developed a routine of support and caring that reflects their own individual lifestyle.

In a Carer's UK survey, *Out of Pocket: A Survey of Carers Lost Earnings* (2007), of around 2,000 carers in England, Scotland and Wales, nearly 10% were from

Most family members will welcome an opportunity to discuss how they would like to be involved in their son or daughter's life, both now and in the future.

minority ethnic backgrounds. This research found that carers from black, Asian and minority ethnic communities were more likely than other carers to say that they were unaware of local services, that services were not sensitive to their needs and that their use of services was limited due to cost or a lack of flexibility. In another Carers UK report, *Support for Black, Asian and Minority Ethnic Carers. A Good Practice Briefing* (2007), they noted that what makes for successful black, Asian and ethnic minority community support for carers is:

- simple clear and accessible information;
- carers involvement in planning, monitoring and evaluation;
- sensitivity to cultural and individual requirements and ability to meet these needs;
- recognition and real commitment from service provider.

Understanding carers' rights and entitlements

Carers were first mentioned in legislation in 1986. In the first 15 years, the legislation focused on how carers should be supported to carry out their caring role: more recently, there is an increasing requirement to view carers as individuals with a right to a life beyond caring and a right to their own support.

Skills for Care and Skills for Health (2011)

The Draft Care and Support Bill (2012) for England gives equal rights to assessment and support for both adults with disabilities and their carers, laying a duty on local authorities to promote the well-being of both.

There are about 6.4 million people in the UK caring for a child, friend, neighbour, partner or parent or a combination of these. Family carers across the UK it is believed save the country about £119 billion in health and social care costs. It is important that family carers are supported to look after their own health and well-being and balance this with the needs of their relative. Many family members are not aware of some of their rights and entitlements, these currently include:

- **Carers' rights to an assessment**

In England and Wales, the Carers (Recognition and Services) Act 1995 and the Carers and Disabled Children Act 2000 give family carers the legal right to an assessment of their needs as a carer if they are aged over 16 and provide a regular and substantial amount of care for someone aged over 18. The Care and Support Act is likely to remove this requirement concerning the amount of care provided. Having their own assessment allows the family carer to meet with a social worker or a health worker to:

- look at what help they need to support them as a carer;
- find out what help and support may be available;
- talk about what plans could be made in planning for the future.

In Scotland the right to a carer's assessment comes under the Social Work (Scotland) Act 1968 as amended by the Community Care and Health (Scotland) Act 2002. In Northern Ireland it is the Carers and Direct Payments Act (Northern Ireland) 2002 that gives family carers a right to a carer's assessment.

- **The Carers (Equal Opportunities) Act 2004**

The Carers (Equal Opportunities) Act 2004 places a duty on local authorities to ensure that all family carers know that they are entitled to an assessment of their needs under the Carers and Disabled Children Act 2000.

This duty arises when the social services department is carrying out an assessment of a person with a disability or planning such an assessment. The carer's assessment should consider supporting the family carer's outside interests including employment, study or leisure.

Country	Relevant legislation
England	The Carers (Equal Opportunities) Act 2004
Northern Ireland	The Carers and Direct Payments (Northern Ireland) Act 2002
Scotland	Scotland: The Community Care and Health Act 2002
Wales	The Carers (Equal Opportunities) Act 2004 (Commencement) (Wales) Order 2005

- **Carers and direct payments**

Direct payments are a way for people to organise their own social care support by receiving funding directly from their council following an assessment of their needs. Family carers often take on the responsibility of ensuring that the direct payments for their relatives are used creatively to provide the support identified in their relative's agreed support plan. In addition a carer can use a direct payment to purchase the services they are assessed as needing to support them in their caring role. This includes support that may help maintain their health and well-being. For example, help with gardening or domestic chores or a short break. They may be charged for services.

- **Carers and employment rights**

The Employment Act (2002), that covers the four UK countries, introduced the legal right to request flexible working for parents of children with disabilities. The Work and Families Act (2006) extended this right across the UK from April 2007 to include carers of adults with disabilities.

There is no absolute right to work flexibly but the law requires employers to consider such requests seriously and any refusal must be due to a clear business case. Family carers also have the right to take (unpaid) time off work for dependants in cases of emergency.

Carers' health needs

A report from Carers Scotland, *Sick, Tired and Caring: The Impact of Unpaid Caring on Health and Long Term Conditions* (2011), found that 96% of respondents said that caring had impacted negatively on their health, with more than a quarter, 27% rating their health as poor or very poor. This was later confirmed in a report *In Sickness and in Health* (2012) where over 8 out of 10 carers described a negative impact on their physical and mental health as a result of caring with 64% identifying a lack of practical support being a contributory factor.

General Practitioners (GPs) have a responsibility to identify patients who are family carers. *Supporting Carers: An Action Guide for General Practitioners and their Teams – 2nd Edition* (2012) is a guide that identifies best practice for GPs; it was published by the Princess Royal Trust for Carers in partnership with the Royal College of General Practitioners. The GP is usually the first point of contact that family carers have with the NHS; and they are ideally placed to provide information, alongside physical and emotional support.

A life beyond caring

Having a life beyond caring can be really important for a family member's wellbeing and self esteem especially if they have been caring for many years. However, maintaining a balance between being a family carer and having time for your own interests and needs can be tricky. Family members themselves may need support or even 'permission' to take time out to do something that they want to do. As a paid worker, you will be well placed to sensitively encourage family members to take time for themselves. The knowledge you have of the local community may enable you to signpost family members to employment, learning or leisure opportunities in the area.

Activity

What services are there for family members in the area where you work? Find out about the local organisations that are able to provide information, advice and support to family carers. Find out what each organisation offers, their contact details, time of opening, etc. Collect together some current and up to date information and decide with a colleague how best you can make this information available to family members and other colleagues should they need it.

Whilst it may not be your responsibility to provide such resources and information, it is important to know what is available and to be able to signpost family members to agencies or voluntary organisations that can offer further information and help.

Some important resources to be aware of include:

- local arrangements for carer's assessments, grants and short term breaks that are available from social services departments;
- local carers centres and services;
- local voluntary groups;
- local Learning Disabilities Partnership Board (in England only);

Having a life beyond caring can be really important for a family member's wellbeing and self esteem.

- national organisations including the National Family Carer Network, Carers UK and the Carers Trust (formerly Princess Royal Trust for Carers and Crossroads Care), Hft Family Carer Support Service;
- Citizens Advice Bureau;
- advocacy organisations, particularly if family carers need support to voice concerns or challenge anything.

The changing needs of family carers

In the same way that the needs of their relative will change over the years, the needs of family carers will change over time too, depending on what is happening in the life of their relative. This is particularly true when family members no longer provide the daily support or care, either because their relative no longer needs their care or because they are receiving it from other people. It may appear that they need little information, however if you are aware of national changes (such as major changes to benefits) or adjustment in your organisation's policies that could affect carers or their relative, do consider passing the information on.

Bear in mind that there are family carers who themselves have a learning disability or autism. They may be supporting partners with a disability or in a mutual caring situation with older family carers in a reversal of roles. Coping with the death of a relative with a learning disability or with the death of a family carer can be emotionally challenging for paid workers, your organisation should provide support in this situation. It can be difficult to know what to say in these circumstances but in listening and 'being there' for people and their memories, you will provide the support required.

Providing accessible resources for family carers

It's said that 'information is power'. If we have good information that is accurate and relevant it can help us make choices and decisions and it's much easier to stay in control. Having to search for information can be both stressful and disempowering. It is essential that information is provided in the right place, at the right time and in the right way.

In *Reaching out to People with Learning Disabilities and their Families from Black and Minority Ethnic Communities* (Poxton et al, 2012), the authors found that whilst there is now more information available, some families are unaware of what support they are entitled to and where to get the information. New interactive websites are not easily accessible to people who do not use English as their first language, or who require support to use computers. One of the people they interviewed said 'To get information is very difficult. You have to be very pushy and scream about what you want. When you have found the information it is good. But to use it is quite difficult.' They identify that family members from black and ethnic minority communities particularly need information that is in an accessible format about:

- how to get a social care or specialist health assessment;
- what is meant by entitlement;
- how arrangements around personal budgets affect people;
- how the benefit system works and how it relates to social care;
- how housing and housing improvement issues are handled.

Providing high quality and accessible information to family carers is part of central government policy in health and social care and a key task of services.

It is especially hard for people with a learning disability, people with autism and family carers to be involved in making decisions at a personal level and at a service development level unless they are well informed. Telling them about the ways they may be able to influence local services is also helpful. They could do this via:

- local authority (England only) Learning Disability Partnership Boards;
- local Health and Wellbeing Boards;
- Healthwatch;
- clinical commissioning groups;
- carers forums;
- patient forums;
- consultations;
- reference groups;
- support groups;
- letters and meetings with councillors and their MP.

Making information accessible

Providing the information required by family members is a skilful task. Not all families will be able to take on board the information that they require at the same pace or in the same way. Some may need information to be given face to face by a paid worker they trust, backed up by written information; others may prefer written or audio information while others may prefer to be given website addresses.

Information is of little benefit if it is provided in ways that are not meaningful to each individual family member. Your knowledge and relationship with the family member will help you to find out the best way for information to be provided.

When making information accessible, remember to:

- write and speak in plain English;
- not use jargon;

- not use acronyms;
- ensure that any written material is in the family carer's first language;
- use interpreter services if the family carer's first language is not English or access telephone interpreting services, in line with your organisation's policies;
- use different formats as appropriate including large print, CD, DVD, photos or pictures;
- address sensory issues through the use of audio CD or DVD, use of sign language or texting;

Your local carers centre may provide support to family carers who have learning disabilities or to people with autism who are also carers.

Determining the best ways of communicating with family members will influence how reviews, meetings and telephone contact are planned. This will help enable family members to be fully involved and to have their views heard and respected.

Thinking point

How will you find out the best way to provide information to the family members that you have contact with? What kind of information helps?

Family carers need information about:

- the organisation's commitment to partnership working with family carers;
- ways in which to prepare for their own needs assessments;
- benefits advice;
- the ways in which person centred planning and support planning takes place and how families are involved;
- how care and support decisions are made and how family carers will be involved;
- how reviews and any formal meetings are made inclusive for family carers, this should include having support available to prepare for any meetings,

including having any documents in advance so that family members can prepare;

- having a named worker they can speak to if there are any issues they need to raise;
- how to raise any issues or concerns about abuse or safeguarding;
- how to make a comment, compliment, complaint or challenge a decision and information about what will happen and when;
- the full range of support and activities available locally and how to access different types of support;
- self directed support, personal budgets and direct payments;
- support from family carer and advocacy groups locally;
- local voluntary sector groups;
- local Learning Disabilities Partnership Boards, and Health and Wellbeing Boards (England only);
- opportunities to become quality checkers.

Challenging discriminatory or inaccessible information

Occasionally you or the family members you are working with may come across some information that is inaccessible for the people it was intended for, or it may be biased or prejudiced in nature. This could be written or verbal information. If this happens your first response might well be to seek clarification, in case there is a misunderstanding or inaccuracy. If it is information that is being provided face to face you could gain clarity by asking: Do you mean...? Are you saying...? Why did you say that? Getting this clarification by questioning the person in a calm and professional manner can be useful as there may have been a misunderstanding. If the information is provided in a written format you will need to go back to the author of the material for clarification.

After seeking an explanation, if you still consider the information to be inaccessible or discriminatory you could consider a number of ways to seek clarification, redress or to report discriminatory information:

- Clearly explain to the person or organisation involved what you find unacceptable and what could make the information better. Don't punish or blame them, rather state clearly what your concerns are and give suggestions on how they might be addressed.

- If the information comes from an organisation you could use their complaints process to highlight your concerns. Most organisations will be happy to provide you with details about their complaints procedure if you can't find it on their website.

- If your concern is about discriminatory information you can get advice from the Equality and Advisory Support Service at the Equality and Human Rights Commission at www.equalityhumanrights.com

- A family carer could seek advice on challenging discriminatory or inaccessible information from one of the national carers' organisations such as Carers UK or the Carers Trust or from their local carers' centre.

- As a support worker you could raise your concerns and seek advice from your line manager or a senior colleague.

Working with family members to access resources

Although you may not have the primary responsibility for providing support to family members, you will nevertheless have a responsibility to signpost them to where they can obtain information and support for their own needs. This means that you will need to know what information and support would be the most helpful for family members and where it is available.

Remember a lot of family members do not feel that they can ask for help and many will have become used to simply coping with their caring role. Sometimes sitting and listening to a family member talking about their situation can be very beneficial for them and may provide you with an opportunity to pass on information about where they can get support. This may be a small carers grant, formal services like short breaks through social services or more informal support from local carers' groups.

It is very important that as a paid worker you are aware of and are sensitive to any cultural and religious differences which affect the needs of people with a learning disability or people with autism from minority ethnic communities and their family members. It is not helpful to make any assumptions based on stereotypes of communities different to your own. Although many of the issues raised will be no different from those of other families, historically service providers have struggled to address different cultural perspectives. It is crucial to be able to overcome any language barriers through the use of interpreters.

> **Thinking point**
>
> *How will you find out about the cultural and religious needs of people with a learning disability and people with autism and their family carers from communities different to your own, in your area?*

Provide feedback to others about the support accessed by family members and any gaps in provision

> When I was ill with cancer the staff really helped me and supported me to see Ceri. I don't know what I would have done without them.
>
> *Christine, Ceri's mum*

Sometimes the support and information that workers provide to a family member is just right, the right pieces of information or advice given at the right time and in the right way. At other times a family carer might ask you something and you don't know the answer, or you pass on some information but it isn't what the family carer wants or needs. Supporting people with autism and people with a learning disability is often busy, even hectic work and there seems to be little time to reflect. However, taking time once in a while to reflect on what has gone well and what has gone not so well can be most helpful and can improve the support you and your colleagues provide in the future.

> **Activity**
>
> *Think about a time you passed on some information or advice to a family member and it was just what the person needed. What made this a good experience for both the family member and yourself? Was it how you both communicated? The relevance of the information? Now think about a time when things maybe didn't go so well, why not? Was it the wrong type of information? Communicated in the wrong way? Not relevant? Discuss your answers with your line manager. Are there any other people you could discuss this with?*

Developing ways of working in positive partnership with family carers will give you opportunities to seek both formal and informal feedback from family members about the support you are providing as well as how you access and pass on information to them. If you identify that the information you are passing on is incomplete, out of date or not relevant to the needs of family carers, you and, if any, the organisation you work for will need to find ways of passing this finding on to the relevant person. This could be a person in your organisation whose responsibility it is to keep information and contact details up to date, alternatively it might be a person in an external organisation. Being family carer aware will make your organisation more attractive to families who are helping their relative manage a personal budget or select who to pay an Individual Service Fund to provide the best support.

If family members are having their own personal difficulties, then this is very likely to have an impact upon their relative. It is important that you have a clear understanding of how far to get involved in and what to do if issues are raised or support is needed that you don't have the knowledge or skills to deal with.

> **Activity**
>
> *Imagine that you are approached by a family carer who is obviously very tearful and upset. She tells you that she has recently lost her part time job and that she is finding it hard to cope financially. In particular, she has not been able to afford to buy a birthday present for her relative, the person that you support, having promised him a day out in London. What would you do?*

There are likely to be times when you support family members either directly or indirectly. You will be ideally placed to identify when things are going well or if family members require additional support. It is important that you always discuss any concerns that you have with your line manager so that shared decisions can be made about what support can be provided by yourself or your organisation. Sometimes it will be appropriate to encourage the family carer to obtain support from their GP, a social worker or community nurse, depending on the issues. This possibility should be sensitively discussed with family members during the initial conversations about roles and responsibilities.

When working out how to respond to a family carer's need for support, remember to consider:

- What is it appropriate for you to do, taking into account your job role and skills?
- Will it have a positive impact on the life of the person you support?
- Who can you discuss any concerns you have with, your line manager or someone else in your organisation?
- Who should make any decisions?
- What information or advice can you provide to enable the family member to receive support?
- Who else should be informed, providing you obtain agreement from the family carer?

Key points from this chapter

- Practical and emotional support, together with accessible information, is vital for family members.
- A supportive partnership relationship with paid staff can be very important for family members and, if you work for an organisation, for its reputation.
- Family members may need help to identify and access support for themselves.

- Paid staff need to know about carers' rights and the local and national support that is available. It is important to discuss any gaps in support with family members to identify ways forward.

- Any decisions should not be made by individual staff members, but should include the advice of a line manager.

References and where to go for more information

References

Carers UK (2007) *Support for Black, Asian and Minority Ethnic Carers. A Good Practice Briefing.* London: Carers UK

Carers UK (2007) *Out of Pocket: A Survey of Carer's Lost Earnings.* London: Carers UK

Carers Scotland (2011) *Sick, Tired and Caring: The impact of Unpaid Caring on Health and Long Term Conditions?* Glasgow: Carers Scotland

Clements, L (2012) *Carers and their Rights: The Law relating to Carers.* Fifth edition. London: Carers UK

Foundation for People with Learning disabilities (2006) *Carers' Assessments – What's in it for you?* Downloadable from: http://bit.ly/T2Vpdi

Hft and Carers Trust (2011) *Reaching and Supporting Diverse Communities: A Guide to Meeting the Needs of People with Learning Disabilities and Family Carers, from Newly Arrived, Black, Asian and other Minority Ethnic (BME) Communities.* Downloadable from: www.hft.org.uk/bmeguide

Poxton, R, Taylor, J, Brenner, D, Cole, A, and Burke, C (2012) *Reaching out to People with Learning Disabilities from Black and Minority Ethnic Communities.* London: Foundation for People with Learning Disabilities

Royal College of General Practitioners and Princess Royal Trust for Carers (2012) *Supporting Carers: An Action Guide for General Practitioners and their Teams.* Second edition. London: Royal College of General Practitioners/ Princess Royal Trust for Carers

Skills for Care and Skills for Health (2011) *The Common Core Principles for Working with Carers.* Downloadable from www.skillsforcare.org.uk

Legislation, policies and reports

All UK legislation can be downloaded from www.legislation.gov.uk

Policies and reports for Northern Ireland, Scotland and Wales can be found at www.northernireland.gov.uk, www.scotland.gov.uk and www.wales.gov.uk respectively. Policies and reports for England can be found on the website of the relevant government department.

Department of Health (2008) *The National Carers Strategy: Carers at the Heart of the 21st Century Families and Communities.* London: Department of Health

Websites

Carers Trust www.carers.org.uk

Carers UK www.carersuk.org

Hft Family Carer Support Services www.hft.org.uk

National Family Carer Network www.familycarers.org.uk

Skills for Care www.skillsforcare.org.uk

Working Families www.workingfamilies.org.uk

Chapter 6

Recording and sharing information together – is the partnership working?

> The email from the regional operational manager of my daughter's service provider after my daughter was unwell:
>
> 'Thanks for the support you have given the staff while Angie was not too well. They have all said that you were really great and really lovely to them.'
>
> My reply:
>
> 'That's nice feedback… thanks for that. It was soooo hard to take a step back, as (the staff) have to learn to 'read' Angie. I asked a few if they now really understood what I meant by that… and thankfully got the affirmatives!!!! Phew!! I think they all realise too that by the time she presents she's poorly, she really is poorly!!!'
>
> *Judi, Angie's mum*

Introduction

This chapter is about the importance of regular, ongoing contact and communication with a person's family members. This should include how their support plan is being put into practice, how any new or changing needs are being listened to and acted upon.

It will also suggest how to record and monitor the progress being made, including how well your partnership with the family members is working. This includes what is happening in relation to any support needs that the family may have at this point in time, for example if there are to be any organisational changes they need to know of.

Reviews and review meetings are helpful in enabling everyone to focus and reflect on how well things are going. This chapter looks at how you can, if necessary, encourage families to take part in the reviews of their relative's support plan. This may mean being flexible and creative to ensure that such meetings are inclusive and support the participation of family members.

Finally this chapter will help you to think about what information you need to share with other professionals about the support needed by family members in their caring role. This will include how family carers might experience discrimination, or difficulties in obtaining accessible information or access to the support or services that they need.

Learning Outcomes

This chapter will help you to:

- exchange information with the person and their family members about:
    - the implementation of the person centred/support plan;
    - any changes in the individual's needs and preferences;
- record information in line with agreed ways of working about:
    - progress towards outcomes;
    - the effectiveness of partnership working with the family carers;
- agree the criteria and processes for reviewing the partnership work with and support for families;
- encourage the person you support and family members to participate in reviews;
- carry out your role in the review of partnership working.

This chapter covers:

Level 3 HSC 3038 – Work in partnership with families to support individuals: Learning Outcomes 5 and 6

Exchanging information with the person you support and their family members

In your role as a support worker you will most likely be exchanging information with the person you support and their family members very regularly. In this section we are focusing on exchanging information about the person's support plan.

The implementation of the plan The person you support should always be in control of their support plan and how it is put into practice. Ideally, the development of the plan will have been completed with the support of family members and paid staff and its implementation will be jointly agreed. This joint approach will help to safeguard ownership of the plan, encourage shared expectations and will provide a focus for the ongoing partnership working with family members as well as others.

As the person's paid worker, you and others may have responsibility for keeping the family members informed about the progress, or any difficulties that arise, in implementing the plan. Being open and honest and having mutual respect will encourage an open dialogue that helps to deal with any difficulties that arise.

Changes to needs and preferences In practice the support plan is a living, organic plan which can be amended at any time to provide better support and direction to meet the person's changing wishes, desires and choices. If such changes do not happen, then the plan is no more than a snapshot in time of what the person wants to do and how they are supported. The support plan should be about living a life and not a plan that gathers dust on a shelf with no impact on the person's life.

> **Thinking point**
>
> *Think about someone you support. How is their support plan presented? Is their plan in a format that is accessible to them and their family members? Is the support plan being followed and how? How are they and their family members involved in continually reviewing and updating their plan? Think of ways to support the person to keep their plan up to date in a way that's meaningful to them and involves their family members.*

Being sensitive to the person's needs and preferences means recording whenever they say or indicate that they want to do something different, go somewhere new or meet someone. They are also likely to be communicating their wants and wishes to their family members which will need to be shared and recognised. Communicating changes in the plan with colleagues, family members and others as needed, and engaging their support to make something happen may mean the difference between the person enjoying an experience they have expressed a wish for and the frustration of not being heard or taken seriously.

If they are not present during a review of the plan, how changes to the plan are communicated to family members should be agreed with the person and their family members at the time that the plan is agreed. It is likely to depend on the nature and significance of the change for that individual as to how far information is just exchanged or whether family members are more involved in deciding how any change is implemented.

The annual social services review of the person's support plan will usually be the responsibility of their care manager or a reviewing officer. But you may play a role in supporting the person to prepare for and lead their review and in ensuring the involvement of family members.

Recording information in line with agreed ways of working

> **Thinking point**
>
> *Think about the records and reports that you have completed or contributed to in your work over the last two weeks. Why was the information collected? Was the person you support involved? How did it contribute to the person's support?*

Workers supporting people with a learning disability and people with autism need to have excellent communication skills. As well as being good at verbal communication you will also need to contribute to written communications such as records and reports. The type of record keeping required will depend on the kind of work you do, the way your service is run and whether you work as a personal assistant. If you work for a large organisation it is likely that you will be required to keep more records than if you are employed by an individual using a direct payment or personal budget. Whether you work for an individual or an organisation you will be required to complete some written reports as part of your work.

When handling information, whether it is recording the use of medication, a support plan or as part of a handover diary you need to keep within the law and follow the policies of your organisation. This will help to ensure information is collected, stored and shared appropriately as well as protecting the privacy of the person you support and their family.

Records should be clear, accurate, complete and up to date.

Activity

Find and read all the policies and procedures in your organisation that relate to handling information. This could include the policies on confidentiality, positive behaviour support, risk management, record keeping and data protection. If you work as a personal assistant your employer may have set out agreed ways of working, that may mean formal policies or procedures, or less formal ways to let their workers know about how they want their support organised. This could be written into your contract of employment or into their support plan or discussed and agreed through your induction and ongoing supervision. When you have read the policies or agreed ways of working talk to your line manager if you have any questions or concerns about how you should be recording and storing information.

When recording information it is important to remember some key principles that include:

- it is presented in a legible and clear manner;
- it is factually accurate, complete and up to date, it contains facts and not opinions;
- the language you use is positive and doesn't use discriminatory language – others may have reason to see your notes in future.

You can find out more about handling information, record keeping, policies and procedures in the book, *Handling Information for Learning Disability Workers* (2011) by Lesley Barcham and Jackie Pountney, another book in this series.

Progress towards outcomes

It's important that progress is recorded in a way that is open and transparent to the person, their family and you and your colleagues. It's important to establish who has responsibility for recording progress and making updates on the support plan.

Thinking point

How would you like to read or see something recorded about you? How would you like it to be recorded?

Activity

You need to do this activity with another person. Spend five minutes telling each other about something you have done and achieved, without taking notes. Then separate and spend five minutes writing up what each of you said without conferring. Then swap your records and look at what each of you has recorded.

Give the recorder marks out of 10 with 1 being poor and 10 being great. Mark it on:

- *how it sounds when read;*
- *the style;*
- *accuracy, how it matches what you said.*

Progress towards the outcomes for the person is likely to happen more effectively if the partnership is working well and if there is an easy flow of communication between you and family members. Any discussions between family members and yourself will help to demonstrate how the partnership is working.

The function of recording goals and achievements in a person's support plan is to show the:

- who;
- what;
- when;
- where;
- how of any outcome from the plan.

This information will be required for the annual review but also to help ongoing monitoring of the person's needs and wishes.

Effectiveness of partnership working Probably the best test of the effectiveness of partnership working between you as a person's paid support worker and their family members is how good a life the person is enjoying. If the partnership is working well:

> **Thinking point**
>
> *What do you think will be the signs that partnership working with family members is working to get the best life possible for the person?*

- the person's voice will be heard and their goals are met;
- new opportunities are presented and enjoyed;
- the interests of the person are consistently at the centre of any discussions and decisions;
- working positively with family members is the established way of working and has led to mutual respect;
- any difficulties are discussed and resolved as quickly as possible.

Agreeing the criteria and processes for reviewing partnership work with, and support for, families

As was explained at the beginning of this book in Chapter 1, partnership working with family members means agreeing:

- how the partnership will work in practice;
- how everyone will know that partnership working is happening and is working well;
- how it will be reviewed;
- how successes will be recorded;
- how any difficulties will be resolved.

As well as face to face, phone or email contact, family members may be kept in touch through a variety of other means that could include informal gatherings, newsletters and meetings.

> **Activity**
>
> *Think about your relationship with a particular family member you work with in terms of mutual respect, listening, power sharing, communication, and integrity.*
>
> - *How many of these characteristics of partnership working apply to this relationship?*
> - *Write down some examples that would provide the evidence that these characteristics are present in your relationship.*
> - *Is there any evidence that show that these characteristics are not present?*
> - *Is your relationship a real partnership?*
> - *What could you **do** to change the relationship into more of a partnership?*
>
> *Discuss your answers to these questions with your line manager or a senior colleague.*

Although the responsibility for a carer's assessment sits with a care manager or social worker, you may be in a good position to know when a family member may be in need of additional support for themselves.

You need to make sure that you know what support is available for family carers in your area so that you can provide information and signposting when required. This could include suggesting that they ask social services for a carer's assessment, providing information about where to get support in relation to benefits or it may be giving the contact details of local voluntary or family-led carers groups.

Encouraging the person you support and their family members to participate in the review of partnership working

Checking that the person you support is happy with the way you, your service and their family is involved in supporting them is important. This needs to be done sensitively and flexibly and involves finding out the views and opinions of the person and their family members.

A review of partnership working doesn't have to be a formal review – but it's important to acknowledge when the review will take place so that family members have time to think about how the partnership is working. If the partnership is working well, then it is likely that all involved will be able to provide many examples of how the relationships have had a positive impact on the person's quality of life.

However, it is likely that the partnership working will be seen as mixed, often working well but with examples of when paid staff and family carers have failed to communicate about particular issues. Having an opportunity to review what has been happening and to agree on ways of learning from what may not have worked is very important.

Activity

Think about a conversation you have had recently with a family member where both of you felt respected, that your views mattered, and where you were able to resolve a difficulty through open discussion and eventual agreement. List three things that you both did that you think contributed to reaching agreement about how to resolve the difficulty. If you think it is appropriate, discuss this activity with the family member and then compare your two lists. What can you learn about how to work together in the future?

Your role in the review of partnership working

I want the staff that support James to put themselves in his shoes and be truly person centred in all that they do. Although everything is written down in James's support plan and they have training from us, his family and their employer they still don't always get it right. Some of the best workers are the ones who ask questions and think about what has gone right and why sometimes things go wrong. As James's mum I am always thinking about his support, reflecting on things, looking for ways to do things differently, better. I want and expect the same from the managers of the organisation that support James and the support workers. Then James gets a good life and he stays safe, healthy and happy.

Tina Cooper, family carer, mother of James

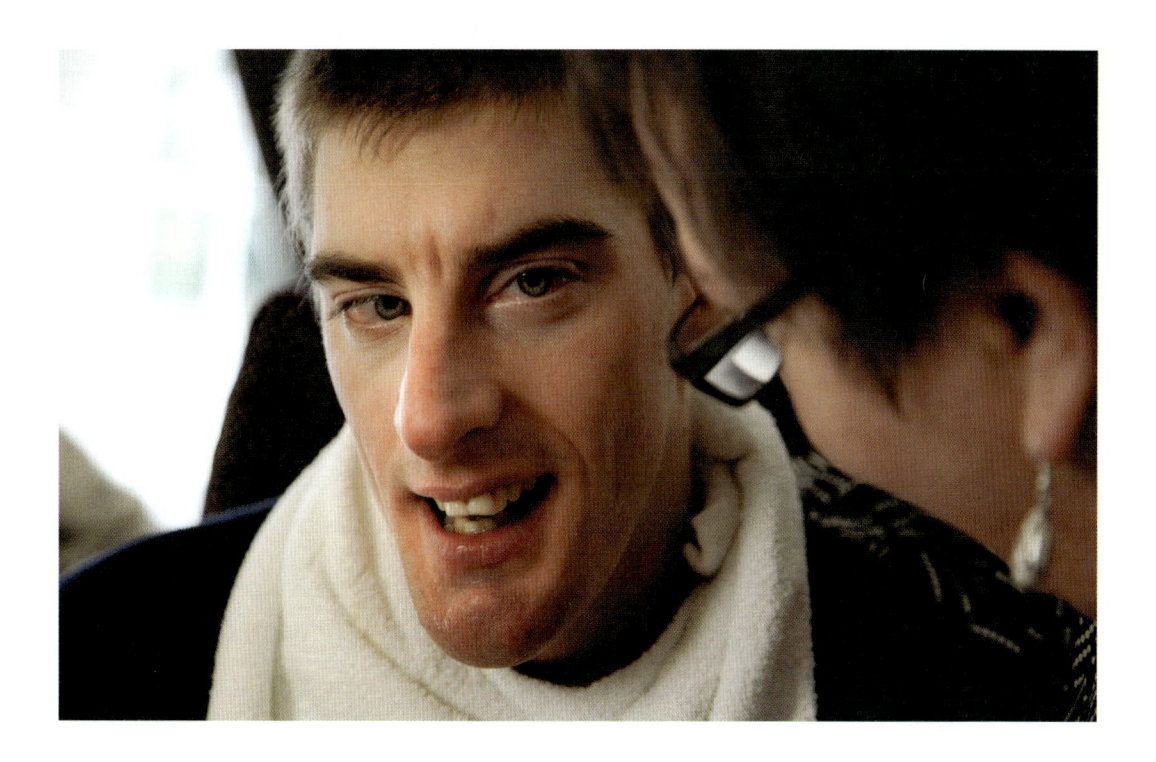

In addition to and separate from any joint review of partnership working, one important way to learn and improve on what you do, whether you are new to supporting people with a learning disability or people with autism, or if you have worked in care for many years is to be a reflective worker. Doing this with a colleague or a family member is an important way to review how the partnership with a family member is doing. Reflection is a way to learn from our past experiences, both good and bad, so that we can get better at what we do. Reflective practice is an organised way to think through, either on your own or with others, what has happened in your support of a person so that you can change things for the better. Reflective practice is practical learning directly from life, not from a book or a course; instead it is learning by taking a new critical look at our own experiences.

Getting into the habit of being a reflective worker from your first days supporting people, then carrying it on throughout your career, will help you to continually learn and improve.

> **Thinking point**
>
> *Think back to one thing that went really well when providing support to a person or a family member in the last week. Now think about one thing that didn't go so well. Why do you think things happened as they did?*

Thinking honestly about what's working and what's not working in terms of how you work with family members is a good way to review your role in partnership working. It may be helpful to discuss this in confidence with a more experienced colleague or your line manager in supervision, and to think about what actions you need to take to improve the effectiveness of partnership working. It may vary from one person's family to another and you will need to think why this might be and what you can do to improve things. Always remember you are seeking solutions, not labelling or stereotyping relatives.

You can find out more about being a reflective worker in the book *Personal Development for Learning Disability Workers* by Lesley Barcham, another book in this series.

Key points from this chapter

- The person you support should always be in control of developing their support plan and putting it into practice.

- The development and implementation of the plan will ideally have been done jointly with paid staff and family members.

- How changes to the plan are communicated to family members should be agreed with the person and their family members at the time the plan is agreed.

- It is important that progress is recorded in a way that is open and transparent to the person you support, their family and to you.

- It is important that information is recorded in line with the policies and procedures of your organisation, or the agreed ways of working with your employer.

- Agreeing criteria for how partnership working will be measured needs to happen when roles and responsibilities are agreed at the start – it's the same in relation to providing support for family members.

- Probably the best test of the effectiveness of partnership working between you as a person's paid support worker and their family members is how good a life the person is enjoying.

- The review of partnership working doesn't have to be a formal review – but it is important to have a shared opportunity for family members and paid staff to reflect on how well the partnership is working and whether any improvements can be made.

References and where to go for more information

References

Barcham, L and Pountney, J (2011) *Handling Information for Learning Disability Workers.* Exeter: Learning Matters/BILD

Barcham, L (2011) *Personal Development for Learning Disability Workers.* Exeter: Learning Matters/BILD

Websites

Carers Trust www.carers.org

Helen Sanderson Associates www.helensandersonassociates.co.uk

Hft Family Carer Support Service www.hft.org.uk

National Family Carer Network www.familycarers.org.uk

PMLD Network www.pmldnetwork.org

Glossary

Advocacy – is taking action to help people say what they want, secure their rights, represent their interests and obtain services they need. Advocates and advocacy schemes work in partnership with the people they support and take their side. Advocacy promotes social inclusion, equality and social justice. People with learning disabilities and family carers can have advocacy support. You can find information about advocacy organisations in your area from Action for Advocacy www.actionforadvocacy.org.uk

Aims – purpose or goals towards which an organisation is working and intends to achieve.

Circle of support – a circle is a group of people who are chosen by someone to support them to achieve their goals in life. See www.circlesnetwork.org.uk for more information.

Communication – the way that two or more people make contact, build relationships and share messages. These messages can be ideas, thoughts or feelings as well as information and questions. Communication involves both sending and understanding these messages and can happen through many different ways including speech, writing, drawing, pictures, symbols, signs, pointing and body language, for example.

Complaint – Any expression of unhappiness, whether spoken or written, from or on behalf of a person about a provider's services, or failure to provide, care and support.

Continuous professional development (CPD) – learning that you undertake after your induction that will help you develop in your role or that will advance your career.

Confidentiality – is an ethical principle that means that information about an individual and their family must be kept private

Direct payments – are made by councils to a person (or a third party 'significant person') who is assessed as needing help from social services, and who prefers to arrange and pay for their own care and support services.

Duty of care – those in a professional or other paid capacity, with responsibility for providing support to others, must take reasonable care to avoid acts or omissions that are likely to cause harm to the person or persons they care for or to another people.

Empower – to enable an individual to take action to control their own lives.

Family carer or family member – a relative or friend of a disabled person who cares for and about them and supports them, so therefore has an interest in their well-being.

Independent living – means disabled people having control and choice over their own lives and their support. See www.ncil.org.uk for more information.

Induction – an introduction and period of learning about a new job, organisation or person and family you are working for and how to work with the people you will be supporting in the best way.

Informed decision – an informed decision is one where a choice is made by someone, using relevant information about the advantages and disadvantages of all the possible courses of action.

Job description – a document that gives detailed information about your job, what you will be doing and who you are responsible to.

Mental capacity – a person's ability to make particular decisions and to understand the consequences of those decisions. Capacity to make a particular decision at a particular time is assessed according to the framework provided by Mental Capacity Act (England and Wales) and its Code of Practice.

The Mental Capacity Act (England and Wales) – is designed to protect people who can't make a particular decision for themselves, ie lack the capacity to do so. This could be due to their age and frailty, a mental health condition or learning disability.

The emphasis is on enabling adults to make as many decisions as they can for themselves with support. For more information see www.scie.org.uk/publications/mca/index.asp

Neglect – systematically and consistently failing to respond to a person's needs or failing to take actions in their best interests. It can be deliberate but is not always done on purpose.

Negligence – failure to use reasonable care that would be expected of any other person in a similar situation.

Person centred working – a way of working with people that enables them to set the agenda on anything to do with their life. Person centred working also includes understanding and managing risk. It means their support is designed with and around them and they are in control of it with the support they need to do this. The person and their dreams are at the centre of everything you do.

Personalisation – means thinking about care and support services from a person's viewpoint. It means starting with the person as an individual with strengths, preferences and aspirations and putting them at the centre of the process of identifying their needs and making choices about how and when they are supported to live their lives. It requires a significant transformation of adult social care so that all systems, processes, staff and services are geared up to put people first.

Policy – a statement or plan of action that clearly sets out an organisation's position or approach on a particular issue and tells staff what should be done in different circumstances.

Power – the ability of a person or group of people to exercise authority over another, thereby controlling and influencing others.

Procedure – a set of instructions which sets out in detail how a policy should be implemented and what staff should do in response to a specific situation.

Reflective practice – being able to reflect on actions you have taken in your work to help you engage in a process of continuous learning.

Rights – a framework of laws that protects people from harm, that sets out what people can say and do and guarantees the right to a fair trial and other basic entitlements, such as the right to respect and equality.

Risk – probability or threat of damage, injury, liability, loss, or other negative occurrence which may be prevented or managed through planned action.

Risk assessment – identifies the risk of potential harm to people including when and why it may happen and the likely consequences. The assessment will look at how best to manage the risk and identify those responsible for managing the risk.

Service – the provision of social care support for a person in their own home, their local community, supported living, a residential home or similar.

Support plan for a personal budget – is used to describe how someone will use their personal budget to be supported. It is written after the self or supported assessment which gives an indicative budget. The support plan has to be accepted by the funding authority under set criteria.

Support plan – is also a detailed plan of a person's support needs that support workers should use to inform their day-to-day support for that individual.

Index

Added to a page number 'g' denotes glossary.

A
accessible information 97–8
'accommodating' approach 60
additional support 113
Adults with Incapacity Act (Scotland) (2000) 28
advice 29
advocacy 119g
agreed ways of working 14, 28
    recording information 109–12
agreements, outcomes of working together 64, 65–74
aims 119g
Assessment Directions 8
assessments, carers' rights to 92
assumptions 30, 33, 90, 101
attitudes
    family carers 14
    of workers 39–41
autism
    family carers with 96
    legislation and guidance 7–11, 28, 53
    need for consistency 56
    supporting people with 41, 49
    uniqueness of individuals 13, 14
Autism Act (2009) 7
Autism Act (Northern Ireland) (2011) 10
The Autistic Spectrum Disorder Strategic Action Plan for Wales 9
'avoiding' approach 60

B
Barcham, Lesley 111, 116
'best interests' decisions 28, 34, 53
black and ethnic minorities 91, 96, 100
Boughton, Tom 49

C
care
    families' contribution to 23–9
    a life beyond 94–5
    managing risk in sharing 79–83
Care Quality Commission 68
carers
    role, in government policy 4–6
    see also family carers

Carers and Direct Payments Act (Northern Ireland) (2002) 92
Carers and Disabled Children Act (2000) 8, 92
Carers (Equal Opportunities) Act (2004) 8, 92
Carers Matter – Everybody's Business 12
Carers (Recognition and Services) Act (1995) 8, 92
Carers Scotland, Sick, Tired and Caring: The Impact of Unpaid Caring on Health and Long Term Conditions 93
Carers UK 90, 91
change 32
Children and Young Persons Act (2008) 8
choice(s) 8, 10, 17, 70, 96
circles of support 17, 66, 119g
citizenship 10
Commissioning Services for People on the Autism Spectrum: Policy and Practice Guidance 9
Common Core Principles for Working with Carers 12–13, 88–9
communication 42, 58, 98, 109, 119g
Community Care and Health (Scotland) Act (2002) 92
community-based support 8
'competing' approach 60
complaint 119g
'compromising' approach 60
confidentiality 36, 68, 69, 119g
conflict and dilemmas 32–8
    principles for addressing 58–9
    ways of handling 59–60
consistency 56
continuous professional development 119g
control 8, 10, 17, 18, 80, 83, 96
cultural practices
    recognising 51
    sensitivity to 100
culture, and exclusion 25

D
Death by Indifference 5–6
decision-making
    exclusion of families from 5

mental capacity 28, 34, 52, 53
shared approaches to 69–71
defensiveness 25, 34
Department of Health 4, 87
dependability, demonstrating 57–8
dialogue 32
dilemmas *see* conflict and dilemmas
direct payments 18, 93, 119g
disabled children, family contribution to care 23–5
discriminatory information, challenging 99–100
Draft Care and Support Bill (2012) 91
duty of care 119g

E
early years, family contribution to care 23–5
empathy 32
Employment Act (2002) 93
empower 119g
empowerment 10
England, legislation and guidance 7–8, 28, 53, 91, 92, 93
entitlements, understanding carers' 91–6
Equal Lives: Review of Policy and Services for People with a Learning Disability in Northern Ireland 10
equal partners 14, 76
Equality Act (2010) 8
Essential Lifestyle Planning (ELP) 77
ethnic minorities *see* black and ethnic minorities
everyday decisions 70, 71
exclusion 5, 25, 68
experiences, recognition of families' 50
experts, family carers as 5, 14, 23–4, 39, 80

F
families
contribution to care and support 23–9
model of the world 36–7
relationships with *see* relationships
supporting when relatives leave home 31–2, 41–2
valuing 16
family carers 2–4
access to support 86
changing needs of 95–6
defined 120g
encouraging participation in reviews 114

exchanging information with 108–9
exclusion of 5, 25, 68
as experts 5, 14, 23–4, 39, 80
feedback from 101–3
with learning disabilities 96
legislation and guidance relating to 7–11, 91–3
a life beyond care 94–5
providing accessible resources for 96–9
role clarification 74–5
understanding rights and entitlements 91–6
working with *see* partnership working
family involvement 68
in best interest meetings 34
factors affecting level of 29–31
managing risk 80
in planning 26–8, 76, 78, 83
service cultures 25
family relationships 16, 34, 50, 52
feedback 55, 83, 101–3
fight for support/services 29
flexible working 93
formal family support 29
Fulfilling and Rewarding Lives: The Strategy for Adults with Autism 7

G
general practitioners (GPs) 93–4
generalisations 90
government policy
caring role 4–6
information provision 96
partnership working 6–12
risk-taking 80

H
Handling Information for Learning Disability Workers 111
Hatton, Sue 49
health needs, carers' rights 93–4
Healthcare for All 6

I
ill health, prevention of 88
In Sickness and in Health 93
inaccessible information, challenging 99–100
inclusion 10, 17

independence 10, 17, 75
Independence, Choice and Risk: A Guide to Best Practice in Supported Decision Making 80
independent living 7, 120g
independent living trusts 29
individual support 10
   see also personalisation
individual(s)
   centrality of 11
   uniqueness of 13, 14
induction 120g
information
   access to 86
   challenging discriminatory 99–100
   exchanging 108–9
   in person-centred plans 66
   private and confidential 36
   provision of 96–9
   recording 109–12
   in support plans 71, 75
   working with families to access 100–1
information sharing 67–9
informed decisions 120g
intentions, recognising 51
An Introduction to Supporting People with Autistic Spectrum Conditions 26–7, 49
Is Information Enough? Exploring the Information Priorities of Families with a Learning Disability from Pakistani Communities 51

J
job descriptions 65, 120g
joint problem solving 60

K
key working 83
knowledge
   of available support 90
   families' specialist 14

L
learning disabled
   encouraging participation in reviews 114
   exchanging information with 108–9
   involvement in planning 28
   involvement in risk assessment 80
   keeping safe and well 72–4
   legislation and guidance 7–11, 28, 53
   parental contribution in the early years 23–5
   respecting wishes and needs of 15
   uniqueness of individuals 13, 14
legislation and guidance 7–11, 53, 91–3
life events 32
line managers 35
listening 17, 100
local authorities, duties 91, 92
love (family) 25, 51

M
major decisions 70, 71
MAP 78
Mencap 5–6, 51
mental capacity 28, 34, 52, 53, 120g
Mental Capacity Act (2005) 28, 34, 120g
mental health 93
Michael, Sir Jonathan 6
models of the world 32–3, 35, 36–7

N
National Carers Strategy: Carers at the Heart of the 21st Family and Community 4–5, 8
National Family Carer Network 3–4
needs
   of carers, changes in 95–6
   of disabled persons
      changes in 108–9
      knowing complexity of 73–4
      respecting 15
neglect 120g
negligence 120g
Next Steps in Supporting People with Autism 49
non-judgemental approach 27
Northern Ireland, legislation and guidance 10–11, 28, 53, 92

O
ongoing feedback 83
openness 55, 111
organisational policies and procedure 35, 68–9, 95, 110
organisational support, supervision 82
Out of Pocket: A Survey of Carers Lost Earnings 90–1

outcomes
   of partnership working, agreeing 64, 65–74
   recording progress of 111–12
partnership working 22
   accessing information 100–1
   agreeing outcomes of 64, 65–74
   attitudes of workers 39–41
   conflict in *see* conflict and dilemmas
   core principles 12–13, 88–9
   demonstrating dependability 57–8
   effectiveness of 112
   policy context 6–12
   reviews
      agreeing criteria and processes for 113–14
      encouraging participation in 114
      workers' role 115–16
   role clarification 74–5
   to identify needed support 87–91

P

PATH (Planning Alternative Tomorrows with Hope) 78
Person Centred Approaches when Supporting People with a Learning Disability 66, 79
person-centred planning 69, 76–8
person-centred plans 65–6, 72–4
person-centred working 9, 36, 75–6, 120g
personal assistants 17, 18, 29, 41, 82
personal budgets 18
   support plans for 78, 121g
Personal Development for Learning Disability Workers 116
Personal Futures Planning 77
personal role clarification 74–5
personalisation 8, 17, 121g
Personalisation: A Rough Guide 17
physical health 93
planned outcomes 64
planning
   family involvement in 26–8, 76, 78, 83
   keeping persons safe and well 72
   personalisation 17
   see also person-centred planning
plans *see* person-centred plans; support plans

policy 121g
   see also government policy; organisational policies and procedures
positive partnership 102
Pountney, Jackie 111
power 121g
power imbalance, carers and paid staff 40
preferences, changes to 108–9
privacy 68
procedure 121g
   see also organisational policies and procedures
progress, recording 111–12
Putting People First 8

R

rapport 55–6
Reaching out to People with Learning Disabilities and their Families from Black and ethnic Minority Communities 96
reassurance 54–5
recognition 49–54, 88–9
recording information 109–12
reflective practice 115–16, 121g
relationships 15
   with families 18
      in the early years 23
      establishing and maintaining positive 46–56
      new 40–1
      power imbalance 40
      principles for addressing dilemmas or conflicts 58–9
   see also family relationships
religious practices
   recognising 51
   sensitivity to 100
resources
   for a life beyond caring 94–5
   see also information
respect 14, 15, 46–7, 88
responsibilities 36, 67, 93, 100, 108
Review of Mental Health and Learning Disability (Northern Ireland) 10
reviews
   of partnership working
      agreeing criteria and processes for 113–14

encouraging participation in 114
worker's role 115–16
of support plans 109
rights 17, 121g
understanding carers' 91–6
risk
defined 121g
managing 79–83
risk assessment 121g
risk-taking 79, 80
roles
agreement of 67
clarification 64, 74–5
reasons for adjustment of 30–1
review of partnership working 115–16
support in carrying out 89–91

S
safety, of disabled persons 72–3
The Same as You? A Review of Services for People with Learning Disabilities 9
Scotland, legislation and guidance 9–10, 28, 53, 92, 93
The Scottish Strategy for Autism 9–10
self-directed support 17–18
Self-Directed Support: A National Strategy for Scotland 10
sensitivity 100, 109
service(s)
culture and exclusion 25
defined 121g
fighting for 29
influencing 97
legislation and guidance 8, 9, 10
unawareness of 91
shared approaches 32, 69–71
Simpson, John 49
Skills for Care and Skills for Health 12, 91
social inclusion 10
Social Work (Scotland) Act (1968) 92
specialist knowledge 14
Statement on Policy and Practice for Adults with a Learning Disability 9
stereotypes 90, 101
stress 58
supervision 35, 82–3
support
agreeing criteria and process for review 113–14
in decision-making 34, 69–71

factors affecting level of family involvement 29–31
families' contribution to 23–9
family carers' access to 86
having to fight for 29
identifying a families' need 87–91
legislation and guidance 7–11
managing risk in sharing 79–83
for persons leaving home 25, 41–2
providing feedback to others about 101–3
role clarification 74–5
self-directed 10, 17–18
Support for Black, Asian and Minority Ethnic Carers. A Good Practice 91
support plans 121g
agreements set out in 67
changes to 109
disabled persons' involvement in 28
implementation 108
information in 71, 75
keeping persons safe and well 72–4
managing risk 81–2
matching process 66
outcomes in 65
for a personal budget 78, 121g
planned outcomes in 64
providing reassurance through following 54–5
reviews 109
role clarification 75
Supporting Carers: An Action Guide for General Practitioners and their Teams – 2nd Edition 93
Sustainable Social Services for Wales – A Framework for Action 9

T
Think Local, Act Personal 8
Tilly, Liz 66, 79
time off work 93
Transforming Your Care (TYC) 11
transparency 55, 111
trust 14, 75

U
unique models of the world 32–3, 35, 36–7
uniqueness of individuals 13, 14

V

values
  person-centred 75
  recognising different 33
Valuing People 7
Valuing People Now 7, 17
view points, recognising different 33–4, 47
A Vision for Adult Social Care: Capable Communities and Active Citizens 8
voice 17

W

Wales, legislation and guidance 9, 28, 53, 92, 93
Work and Families Act (2006) 8, 93
working together *see* partnership working